I Walked From
Land's End To John o' Groats

Front cover illustration:

View from the northern end of Glen Quaich (Tayside Region) with Loch Freuchie in the background.

I Walked From
Land's End To John o' Groats

A Walker's Guide

KRISTER ANDRÉN

The Pentland Press
Edinburgh – Cambridge – Durham – USA

First published in 1998 by
The Pentland Press Ltd.
1 Hutton Close
South Church
Bishop Auckland
Durham

British Library Cataloguing in Publication Data.
A catalogue record for this book is available
from the British Library.

ISBN 1 85821 565 X

Typeset by Carnegie Publishing Ltd
Carnegie House, Lancaster

Printed and bound by Antony Rowe Ltd. Chippenham

To my patient family
Maj, Mona and Ulf

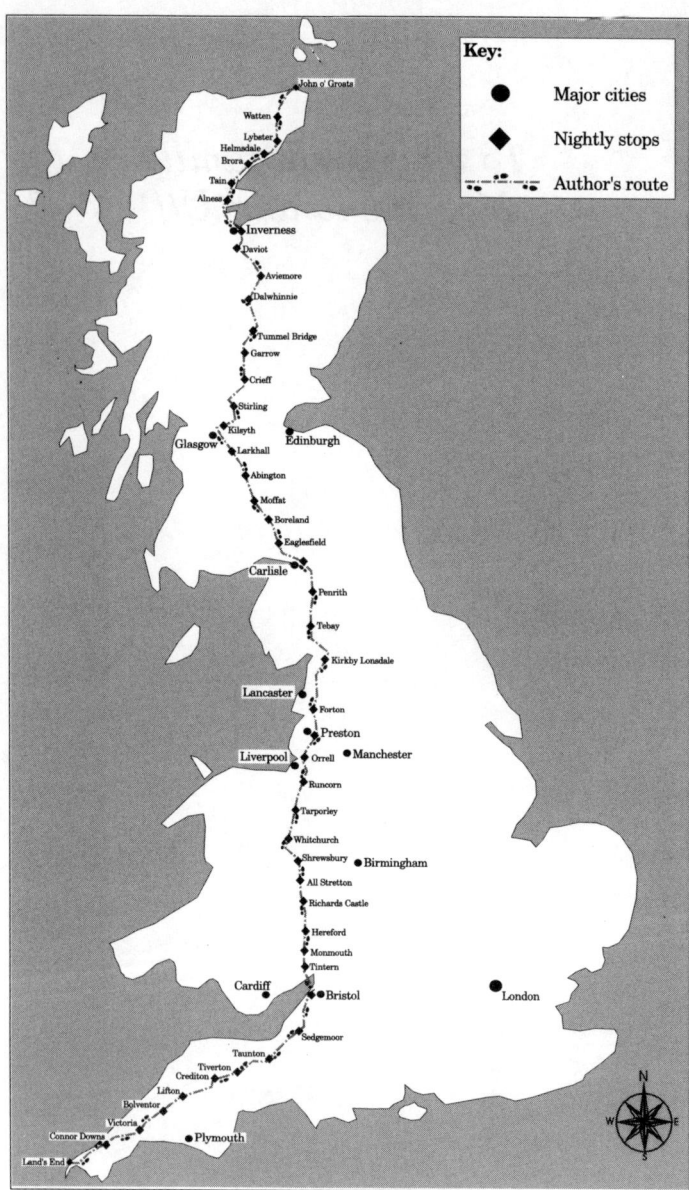

Key:

● Major cities

◆ Nightly stops

Author's route

John o' Groats
Watten
Lybster
Helmsdale
Brora
Tain
Alness
Inverness
Daviot
Aviemore
Dalwhinnie
Tummel Bridge
Garrow
Crieff
Stirling
Kilsyth
Glasgow   **Edinburgh**
Larkhall
Abington
Moffat
Boreland
Eaglesfield
Carlisle
Penrith
Tebay
Kirkby Lonsdale
Lancaster
Forton
Preston
Liverpool   Orrell   ● **Manchester**
Runcorn
Tarporley
Whitchurch
Shrewsbury   ● **Birmingham**
All Stretton
Richards Castle
Hereford
Monmouth
Tintern
● **Cardiff**   ● **Bristol**   ● **London**
Sedgemoor
Taunton
Tiverton
Crediton
Lifton
Bolventor
Victoria   ● **Plymouth**
Connor Downs
Land's End

N
W   E
S

vi

Contents

Contents

Introduction

The two points on the British mainland which are most remote from each other are Land's End at the tip of Cornwall and John o' Groats tucked away in the north-east corner of Scotland. This is the ultimate walk in Britain. The distance, according to the signposts, is 874 miles (1,406 km) but it can be much longer if you choose minor roads or footpaths.

This classic 'End to End' journey, which holds a certain fascination for many people, has a long history but the walk became more widely known in early 1960 when Dr Barbara Moore completed the walk in 23 days, on a vegetarian diet. Her achievement was much publicized and in February the same year a foot-race from north to south was organized by Billy Butlin. As many as 4,000 people responded to the advertisement, 1,500 sent in entry forms and 715 showed up for the start. Weather conditions were bad and only 138 reached the goal. This says something about the difficulty of the task.

Most journeys are made by bicycle, no doubt because it is difficult to cover the distance on foot within a normal annual holiday. Some people seem to be driven by a desire to be the first to make the journey in an original manner. A few examples: Two brothers-in-law took turns pushing each other in a wheelbarrow! A gentleman from India ran the distance – backwards! Someone has rollerskated the whole way! Then there are the record breakers. In 1995 Richard Brown walked/ran from south to north in 10 days, 2 hours and 25 minutes. His daily distance equalled about three marathon races. And he did it for ten consecutive days! On the same occasion his wife Sandra broke the women's record and clocked in at 13 days, 10 hours and 1 minute. It is true that they found a route which reduced the

1

distance to 830 miles, had a large organization and vehicles with support teams and a £10,000 budget, even so, an incredible endurance feat by both of them but it must have been more pain than fun.

Actor Joss Ackland is probably personally responsible for more blisters and other foot problems than anyone else I can think of. In the television programme *The First and the Last*, which was shown around 1990, he played a recently retired gentleman who decided to walk from Land's End to John o' Groats. He experienced a great deal of hardships on the way but still managed to inspire many to attempt the journey. If I had not watched the programme, I may not have become aware of the challenge.

When I decided to take on the walk, I had, like Joss Ackland's character, recently taken (early) retirement, so I was certainly not out to break any records, nor to use bizarre means of transportation. I have a long-standing affection for Britain and wished to see more of the country at a more leisurely pace than during several previous holidays by car. There may also have been an element of wanting to prove to myself that I was capable of an effort of this magnitude (the retirement syndrome?) and perhaps also of needing a civilized adventure.

I began preparations and did the walk by road, solo and without backup, in two parts. I started from Land's End on 23rd February, 1996, hoping to complete the journey in April, but this was not to be. A severe inflammation of my right Achilles tendon forced me to discontinue the walk after only ten days (in Tintern). This injury was in all probability caused by the fact that on the second and fifth days I walked (and even jogged part of the way to find accommodation before dark) 31 and 33 miles (50 and 53 km), respectively, far longer than I had planned. This was due to inexperience, but I could not anticipate the

2

consequences, not having had any tendon problems before. However, I have to admit that I had only once before done a similar mileage – in the military service, more than 40 years ago! To continue was out of the question, especially as I had most of the journey still ahead me and, on doctor's advice and in utter disgust with myself, I travelled home to heal the injury.

Not willing to give up, however, I restarted from Tintern on the 14th October and did reach John o' Groats on the 19th November after a total of 46 days on the road. There were actually 47 calendar days but the first day (start at 12.10 p.m.) and the last day (I clocked in at the Post Office in John o' Groats at 11.20 a.m.) of the second part of the journey were only half days. I also took a day off so the real time was 45 days. In the chapter 'Road Directions' I have listed 46 consecutive walking days.

A journey of this magnitude should be carefully planned. Not only will this make your walk smoother and help avoid unpleasant surprises but also the planning itself and the anticipation of the many delights awaiting you will bring almost as much enjoyment as the feat itself. You can spend many happy hours poring over the maps and studying the wealth of opportunities.

The books I consulted during my preparations provided very little practical information. Surprisingly little seems to have been written about the 'End to End' journey and even less about roadwalking. My ambition with this little book has not been to write an entertaining narrative about my exploits, but rather to share with potential 'End to End' walkers, who may not have done any ultralong distance walks, my experiences and views on a number of practical aspects and, hopefully, to help avoid some pitfalls.

Selection of Route

The choice of route is of course individual, depending on special interests and places to visit. If you wish to use a fairly direct route, there are really only a few major strategic decisions to make (going from south to north):

1) After Bristol you can either choose to a) cross the Severn Bridge and go straight north to the Lake District, or b) continue north-east and through the Birmingham area and the Peak District to the Lake District. 2) After Carlisle you can go north by way of Hawick, Galashiels, Edinburgh and Perth to Inverness, or 3) go north-west and before reaching Glasgow you can decide either a) to continue through Glasgow and along Loch Lomond to Fort Williams and north-east along Loch Lochy and Loch Ness, or b) go north to Stirling and the Grampian Mountains to Inverness.

The best thing to do is to obtain a small scale map and plan your overall strategy. A road atlas will also be useful. Then get large scale maps to cover the first third of the walk. The rest can be purchased as you go along or you can perhaps arrange for someone to mail them to you. See also the chapter 'Maps and Navigation'.

The Land's End – John o' Groats Association has a Route Advice Service which I strongly recommend. If you specify a number of places you wish to visit, they can provide a suggested computer planned route, avoiding dangerous and known problem roads. This material specifies road numbers, distances, directions and signpostings. The cost for this service is very reasonable. If you wish to use it, write to **Colin Jones, 33 Constance Road, Northwick, Worcester, WR3 7NF.**

Maps and Navigation

The road system is dynamic and subject to constant changes. Reality may not always conform to your maps. Make sure that your maps are recently published. Ask local people about your route for the next few days.

For roadwalking the 1:50,000 scale is adequate and the Ordnance Survey Landranger maps are superb. There are also 1:25,000 Pathfinder maps but you do not really need all that detail and, furthermore, they mean more maps and bulk to carry. I used 38 maps. I brought the first dozen maps with me and bought the rest as I went along. I sent home maps in batches of 5-8 to keep the bulk down. If you wish to follow my route, here are the OS 1:50,000 Landranger map numbers: **203, 204, 200, 201, 191, 192, 181, 193, 182, 172, 162, 149, 138, 126, 117, 108, 102, 97, 90, 91, 85, 79, 78, 72, 71, 64, 57, 58, 52, 42, 35, 36, 27, 26, 21, 17, 11, 12.**

For the inexperienced map-reader it is useful to learn the basics and also to study the signs and abbreviations explained on the maps. E.g. pylons, public houses and even public telephones can be valuable navigational aids. It is important to be able to estimate distances and it is useful to know that the thin blue lines in the grid system on the 1:50,000

maps are spaced at one km (about 0.6 mile) intervals (2 cm on the maps). For quick reference, it may also be helpful to know what the length of your thumb or the space between thumb and little finger, when you spread your hand on the map, represent in terms of distance. You should also bring a distance meter, an instrument with a little wheel which you roll on the map along your intended route. See illustration.

When to go?

The winter season should be avoided for obvious reasons – some roads in northern Scotland may be closed by the police owing to snow.

I personally feel that the summer period may not be ideal as it can be unpleasant to walk in warm conditions, and the roads will probably be busier and competition for accommodation stronger. There may also be a problem with the irritating midges in Scotland in the summer months.

In my opinion the best time to do the walk is during the cooler periods of March–May and September–October, when you will perspire less, feel more energetic and be able to walk faster. However, the summer period does have the advantage of longer daylight, making it possible to do the daily mileage at a leisurely pace.

North or South?

There are good reasons for starting at Land's End. The prevailing winds in Britain are south-westerly and will push you on. This is a not insignificant factor, although you will certainly also encounter other wind directions. I did face some very persistent northerly winds. Also, sun and rain will not be in your face. On the other hand, some people I talked to said that north to south seemed easier, as it felt like walking downhill!

If you walk in the spring, the climate will be on your side, if you start at Land's End. If you start very late in the year, it is probably better to begin from John o' Groats.

In addition, for me at least, John o' Groats, being more remote and perhaps therefore more romantic, seems to be the more appealing place to complete the journey.

Walking solo or with friend/s?

During the walk you will be cut off from your family and normal social network for a long period of time, excepting of course telephone calls. A solo walk over several weeks can therefore be a trying experience psychologically. Doing the walk with friend/s will ensure that you have a conversation partner and someone to do the planning with. You can also share some of the equipment, e.g. maps.

It is important that you and your walking companion/s are compatible and can put up with each other for such a long time. As someone has said: 'Friends are like fish – after three days they begin to smell'. You should also be well matched as regards walking speed and stamina and be able to agree on the choice of route and things to do and see. This is a rather tall order but if you have a friend or friends with the desired characteristics, and sufficient time at their disposal, a joint walk is probably a good idea. Alternatively you could invite friends to join you for parts of the journey.

I did the walk solo and even if I am not the overly gregarious type, I have to admit that there were a few times, during non-walking hours, when home-sickness made itself felt. But mostly one is kept busy finding food, studying the maps, making notes in the diary etc. On the other hand, I was my own master and did not have to show consideration to anyone or to make compromises.

In retrospect I am glad that I walked solo. It would have been embarrassing to abandon a co-walker, as my injury would have forced me to do. I have not seen any statistics but suspect that quite a few walk-ers fail to complete the journey. For this reason, if you do not walk solo, there should perhaps be at least three walkers.

Physical Fitness

Unless you frequently go for long walks and are physically very fit, a long period of preparation is advisable to avoid unnecessary problems which might jeopardize your journey. Assuming that you are not in great shape, a period of 4-5 months would be ideal to tone up your body and toughen your feet. Start by doing brief walks, e.g. 5-7 miles every sec-ond day over the first few weeks and increase gradu-ally the daily mileage until you can walk the desired distance without feeling exhausted. After 3-4 months do the full mileage on several consecutive days to ensure that you can take it. See also the chapter 'Walking Technique'. Take it easy during the last week or so before the start of your 'End to End' jour-ney. Go only for short walks and recharge your bat-teries.

I estimate that I did some 300 miles (around 500 km) in preparation for the first part of the walk and perhaps 200 miles (around 300 km) for the second part.

It is important that you get used to transporting the equipment you plan to bring. If you decide to use a rucksack, this makes a lot of difference compared to using a trolley (see the chapter 'Rucksack or Trolley?'). Do your preparatory walks under field conditions to avoid surprises when doing the real thing.

Not everyone will have the time and patience for a long preparation period. The absolute minimum would be to put in a sufficient mileage to make sure that your footwear suits you perfectly and let the walk itself be the training period. It may then be sensible to keep to a restrained mileage initially and increase gradually. A day off every week is probably also a good idea.

Foot Care

Your feet are the most important part of your body on a marathon walk like this. At best your feet will feel well-used and sore during the first few weeks of the walk, even with preparatory walks back home, but, with luck and good care, they will not give you any problems during the rest of the walk.

I did not have a single blister or other serious foot problem throughout the journey. However, not many walkers are so fortunate. There are examples of the most painful blisters, open wounds, and lost toenails which can turn the walk into a nightmare of heroic suffering and, indeed, even make further progress impossible. With proper preparations, good shoes and foot care much of this is avoidable. Whenever your feet give the slightest signals of discomfort, stop and try to diagnose the cause, which may simply be a small pebble or a wrinkled sock. If there are spots on your feet that you know to be sensitive, tape them to reduce friction. Prevention is always better than cure. If you feel that a blister is developing, tape the area immediately or, better still, use a thick plaster or a piece of adhesive moleskin, in which you cut out a hole of suitable dimension to relieve pressure. Visit your pharmacy and buy an assortment of plasters to have in readiness on the journey.

Examine your feet daily and pamper them. Use a foot-balm or moisturising cream to protect your feet against friction and rubbing and to keep the skin smooth. Apply every morning and night but not on spots which you will tape, as this will reduce adhesion. If you use a foot-file, do so with a light hand. The thick skin under the feet is there for a purpose.

Footwear

During the 'End to End' walk you will probably take some two million steps. The daily pounding over a long period of time is considerable and the choice of footwear is therefore critical.

Should you use heavy walking boots, sturdy walking shoes, lightweight walking shoes or trainers? Boots with high cuffs may be necessary if you walk in rough terrain but they are heavy and not necessarily required for roadwalking. One boot can weigh around two pounds whereas the lightweight shoe I used weighed ¾ pound. This means that with boots you would have to shift more than two million pounds extra! Trainers are light and feel comfortable but may not give the feet sufficient support for such a long walk but it might be a good idea to bring a pair for evening use. I would recommend using walking shoes and the ones I chose were light, had soft leather and good shock-absorbing properties. Oddly enough, they were fairly inexpensive, less than £50.

There are so-called waterproof shoes on the market and they may be effective, at least in light rain. However, in strong winds when the rain comes at you almost horizontally, the water will find a way into your shoes anyway. These shoes are said to 'breathe', i.e. let out moisture from the feet. This may be true to a certain extent but in warm conditions these shoes will probably make your feet feel more clammy than if you are using ordinary shoes. The waterproof shoes I tried were rather heavy and stiff but they may be suitable for other walkers.

Non-waterproof shoes should be treated with boot-wax to make the leather water-resistant and soft.

I also tried using pull-on rubber galoshes but they were uncomfortable to walk in, slowed me down and anyway would not give sufficient protection in rain combined with strong winds. The only way to ensure dry feet is to use wellingtons but they are heavy, bulky and totally unsuitable to walk in for any distance.

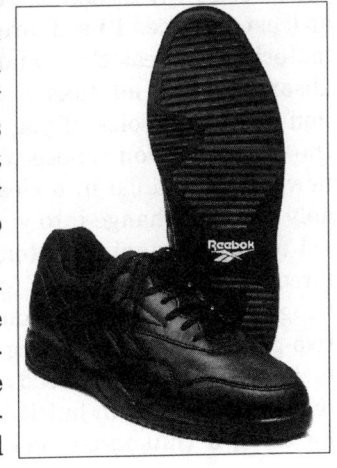

Shoes which feel comfortable and snug in the shop may cause problems when you have walked in them for several miles. To avoid bruised toenails it is especially important that the size of the shoes does not allow the toes to come into contact with the front of the shoes, not even in a descent, when the feet slide forward inside the shoes. One must also allow for the fact that the feet will swell, when hot.

Test the footwear thoroughly during your physical preparations. Do not start the walk with shoes that do not feel completely comfortable. Try others until you are satisfied. This is a key factor for a successful attempt at the 'End to End' walk.

One pair of shoes will probably not last the whole distance. You will need at least two pairs and it might be prudent to have a third pair in reserve at home to be sent to you, if needed. All shoes should be properly broken in before the walk.

Your feet may not give you any problems in your everyday activities but pronation or supination may be critical in a walk of this magnitude. I suggest that you visit early in your preparations a specialist who can detect a potential problem and provide individually moulded support insoles. This may be one of your better investments. Furthermore, these soles, at least the ones I used, are made of non-absorbent material, whereas the standard soles in some shoes absorb water and take a long time to dry. With non-absorbent soles, if you get soaked, you can dry the insides of your shoes with a piece of cloth or a newspaper, change into clean socks and be reasonably dry – or change into your extra shoes.

I used high quality cotton tennis socks with reinforced zones. I brought four pairs with me and bought more en route. Some walkers prefer using two pairs of socks to reduce friction and give a comfortable feeling. The disadvantage is that your feet may get quite warm but this can perhaps be helped by using a thin inner sock. There are also double socks on the market. I tried these during my preparations but found it very difficult to put them on without wrinkles, which may cause blisters.

Whatever method you choose, do your experimenting before you start the actual walk. Experiments en route may give you serious problems and even force you to discontinue the journey.

Clothing

Use comfortable and loose-fitting clothes. Avoid denim jeans. They are rough and may chafe. They are also heavy, especially if they get wet, and take a very long time to dry. I used lightweight cotton trousers which can be unzipped at mid-thigh and converted into shorts, an ingenious feature which I did not use very often, as it happened. You may find it practical to use a thigh-length jacket with many pockets.

Although you should avoid walking after dark, it is safest to sew reflecting bands onto your trousers and jacket to increase your visibility to motorists, just in case.

One other thing – even if you do not normally use a belt, do bring one with you. The 'End to End' walk does things to your waistline.

Laundry

I brought sachets of detergents and did my washing once a week or so in a basin and dried the garments overnight. It is of course possible to hunt down laundrettes but I did not find it necessary.

Rainwear

The rainwear I brought proved to be inadequate for anything but light rain. Consequently I was soaked on several occasions in the heavy rain and strong winds I encountered during the second part of my journey. I finally bought a new set but the hard-won experience taught me that the choice of rainwear (trousers and jacket with a hood) is important.

Many manufacturers claim that their product is waterproof but this may be exaggerated. The material itself should obviously be waterproof but it is equally important that the seams are taped to keep water out.

Choose a material which is lightweight but not flimsy. Avoid heavy materials. Test the rainwear with a handshower in your bathroom. If it is permeable, claim your money back and buy rainwear of another make until you are satisfied.

One disadvantage with waterproof rainwear is that body vapour cannot escape easily and you may feel a bit clammy after a while. However, this is preferable to getting thoroughly soaked with rain. It is of course vital that the rainwear should have a hood.

Rainwear is necessary not only in rain; it is equally useful to protect you from getting cold in strong winds by preserving body heat.

Rucksack or Trolley?

A rucksack may seem the natural choice for transporting your equipment but if you do not have any backup, it will probably weigh so much that after

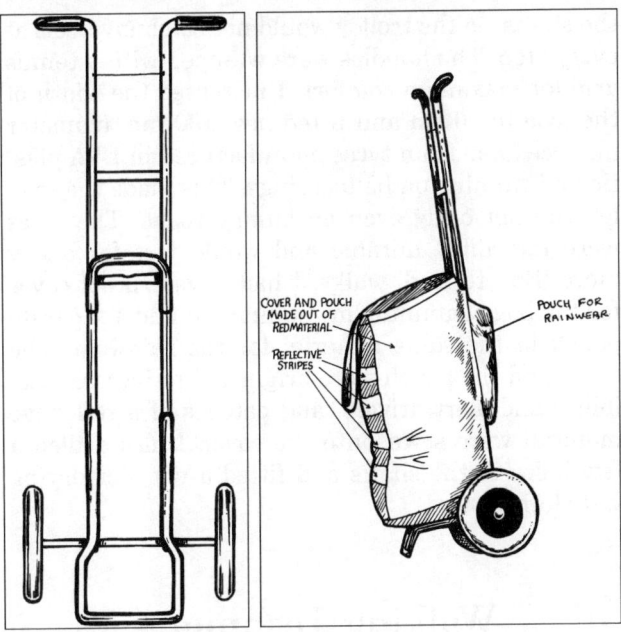

COVER AND POUCH MADE OUT OF RED MATERIAL

REFLECTIVE STRIPES

POUCH FOR RAINWEAR

a long day's walk you will feel very tired. Some people are capable of carrying heavy packs on their backs over long distances, but, if you are walking by road, there is little point in being a beast of burden, so I chose to use a trolley. My equipment, including the trolley, weighed around 28 pounds (plus another four pounds for food and drink) and I hardly felt the weight, except perhaps when going uphill. I often switched hands but, whenever there was traffic, kept the trolley as a buffer between me and the cars. I believe that a trolley is the best choice for the road-walker.

There was no suitable standard trolley on the market so I used a sturdy shopping trolley, inherited from a very sweet, nonagenarian aunt of mine. Sadly, she never knew the good use it was put to. I rebuilt it to suit my purposes. (See illustrations.) I prolonged the shafts, so the trolley would not catch my heels at every step. The handles were wrapped with a tennis grip for maximum comfort. I increased the width of the axle to 50 cm and fitted new 190 mm diameter microcellular foam tyres manufactured in EVA plastic and running on ballbearings. This made the trolley run smoothly even on bumpy roads. The tyres were incredibly durable and would last for a few more 'End to End' walks. I had a waterproof cover for the bag containing my equipment and a separate pouch in the same material for the rainwear. The cover and the pouch were bright red to increase visibility and alert drivers, and patches of a reflective material were sewn onto the cover. I also drilled a few holes in the shafts and fitted a wire for drying wet clothes on.

Walking Technique

Daily mileage is highly individual and dependent on your fitness and the time you are prepared to spend on the journey. Most walkers seem to fall in the range of 20-40 km (13-25 miles) a day. Your pre-walk training will indicate which mileage you are comfortable with. It is natural to feel tired after a day on the road but you should not feel drained. If you overdo it, and press your body too hard, the risk of injuries will increase. I am speaking from personal and bitter experience.

Walking speed also varies considerably and the range is usually between 4-7 km (2.5-4.3 miles) per hour. Again it is important not to overdo it. Do not walk so fast that you get winded and too tired. It is possible to perform over one's capacity for several days but on a walk of long duration this is to invite trouble.

The speeds mentioned above refer to walking on roads without steep gradients. It is easy to believe that uphill and downhill will in the end cancel each other out but this is not so. When ascending, shorten your stride and reduce your speed so you do not get winded and too hot. A good ascent may reduce your speed by half or more. Having negotiated the ascent, you may feel a bit tired and wish to take it easy for a while. Apart from that, to compensate for the loss uphill, you would have to increase your speed by 50% or more over a corresponding distance and this is hardly possible without jogging. So, in hilly areas your speed and daily mileage will obviously decrease.

It is very useful to know your walking speed. I found during my preparations that my normal walking speed on flat ground was 6 km (almost 4 miles) per hour. 5 km (about 3 miles) per hour was a relaxed pace. My overall effective walking speed throughout the journey, taking into account ascents, poor roads and adverse weather conditions was probably 5 km per hour. Knowing such key figures makes it easier to plan the walk and by checking on the map the distance to the next road, you will know when to start looking for it.

A total effective walking time of 5-7 hours is probably a suitable daily dose for most walkers. If you walk late in the year, it is important to know e.g. that there are only about eight hours of daylight in Scotland in November. Try to avoid walking on roads after dark as your reduced visibility to motorists can cause dangerous situations.

Some walkers prefer to walk almost continuously with very few breaks while others may wish to stop frequently to rest or to enjoy scenery etc. This depends to a certain extent on weather conditions.

When I did the walk (the second part was in October-November), it was often quite cold and the breaks tended to be very short. I often had to keep walking to generate body heat and feel comfortable.

Under good conditions I would prefer the following pattern: After stretching exercises, make an early start and walk slowly for the first 15 minutes or so until you feel warm and then continue at a good pace and take a 10-15 minute break after about two hours. Then walk for another two hours before stopping for lunch for an hour or so. You should by now have covered about two thirds of the day's mileage and have an easy afternoon's walk to reach your destination in good time. During breaks and at the end of each day's walk, repeat the stretching exercises.

I have always thought that people look a bit silly when doing these exercises, seemingly bent on trying to push down the houses or trees or whatever they are leaning against. However, I have been assured that stretching can help prevent injury to muscles, tendons and ligaments. After my early injury I was prepared to try anything, so during the second part of the journey I did the exercises – but surreptitiously.

You may find it worthwhile to use a pedometer, an instrument which automatically counts your steps. There are advanced models which, set to the average length of your stride, transfer your walking motions onto a scale, enabling you to read the distance covered. See illustration.

The mileages indicated in the 'Road Directions' do

not necessarily mean that I walked these distances on the given days. As it was not always possible to find accommodation at suitable intervals, the distances varied considerably. To avoid high mileages I sometimes used the following method:

If a short day was followed by a long one, I walked for an hour or two beyond the first day's destination, having first arranged with my hosts or a taxi to fetch me at an agreed place, bring me back to the B&B, and to return me to the same spot the next day. This worked very well and often made it possible to avoid high mileages. If I had been sensible enough to think of this possibility in the early stages of my walk, I could probably have avoided the injury that forced me to do the walk in two parts.

Road Sense

Motorways are of course out of the question as it is illegal to walk on them. Other major roads should also be avoided, at least when there are alternative minor or local roads, which do not involve considerable detours. However, there are occasions when major roads cannot be avoided. This is the case especially in northern Scotland, where there are few alternatives to the A9. Regarding major roads I feel that those with dual carriageways are safer, as you do not have to consider traffic from the rear.

When walking on roads without footpaths your exposure to traffic will obviously increase the risk factor, as compared to walking off-road. While many roads, especially near more densely populated areas, provide footpaths and many roads have hard shoulders, of varying width and quality, the roadwalker will often have to share the road with the motorised traffic. It is necessary to be alert at all times and to be aware of the risks.

The ground rule, in a country with traffic on the left, is of course to walk on the right-hand side of the road so that you face the oncoming traffic and can take evasive action, if needed. However, there are some situations when one should consider crossing over to the left-hand side. The two obvious situations are when you approach a blind bend or a blind crest, where the motorists will not be able to see you before they are almost upon you. Some roads are unfortunately such that it is impossible to step off them. In these cases it is courting danger not to cross over to the other side. This should be done with extreme care and at a safe distance from the bend or crest and with attention to traffic coming from the rear. When you have passed the bend or crest and can check the traffic in both directions, cross back quickly.

Another situation when it may be prudent to walk on the left-hand side is when a low sun shines into the eyes of drivers of oncoming vehicles and may make it difficult for them to see you. These situations may not only be dangerous to the walker but also to motorists if the driver makes a sudden panicky manœuvre when spotting you.

Most drivers, especially professional ones, are quite considerate and usually give you a wide berth but this may not always be possible because of oncoming traffic. A special problem is that large vehicles can produce a strong slipstream which, if close, can almost stop you in your tracks. In these cases it is best to step off the road.

If you see oncoming traffic and at the same time can hear vehicles coming from behind, take a look and if the cars are likely to meet near the spot where you are, step off the road, if possible.

The main risk with roadwalking is when a driver

coming from behind overtakes a car and the three of you meet. Your ears cannot detect this situation and on a narrow road the overtaking car will be uncomfortably close. These drivers are not only inconsiderate but also dangerous and, in my opinion, should be relieved of their driving licences – if they have one. However, since such drivers do exist, I recommend that, at the risk of dislocating your neck, you cast a look whenever hearing traffic approaching from behind. You should also walk as far out on your side of the road as possible at all times.

It may be tempting to listen to music or the radio, using a walkman with earpiece. Do not do it on roads without a footpath! This is highly dangerous as you will not get early warnings from the traffic.

Nutritional Aspects

The average energy intake of an adult male without strenuous occupation is usually around 2,200–2,400 kcal per day, corresponding to 100 kcal per hour. It has been estimated that walking at a normal pace requires 0.08 kcal/min/kg which, for a bodyweight of e.g. 74 kg (163 lbs), corresponds to about 350 kcal per hour. This amount will increase if you walk fast, carry equipment and also if you are exposed to low temperatures. So the energy expenditure increases by a minimum of about 250 kcal per hour over and above the normal rate. A six-hour walk thus increases the energy requirement by an extra 1,500 kcal, and probably considerably more!

Experience shows that it is difficult to compensate for this extra requirement. You will burn more energy than you eat and walkers have reported weight losses of up to 16 pounds during the journey despite eating more than normally. While few people would mind losing excess weight, the 'End to End' walk is hardly the time for a slimming programme. It is important to eat properly with a varied diet and consume plenty of energy-giving foods during a physical exercise of this magnitude and for many it may be a blessing to be able to eat ad libitum without paying the penalty (but one must not forget to reduce the intake at the end of the walk).

I tried to keep to the following schedule: A full cooked breakfast with juice, cereals and milk, tea and toast with marmalade, and bacon and eggs. The lunches tended to be light – often a bar meal or sandwiches I had brought. A solid dinner, when I could find it, which was far from always, whenever possible with pasta which contains slow carbohydrates. In between these main meals I munched chocolate bars, bananas and other fruit, ginger biscuits etc. In spite of all this, I lost weight at the rate of two pounds per week.

It is also important to pay attention to the fluid balance. It is obvious that in warm conditions you need to drink more but even at cooler temperatures perspiration will increase. You will probably need 1-3 litres extra per day. Always carry a large plastic bottle with water or soft drink and take frequent sips.

If it is very warm when you walk and you perspire a lot, it may be advisable to use salt tablets.

Accommodation

On a journey of long duration it is neither practical nor necessary to book accommodation in advance for the entire journey. The marvellous B&B system combined with guest houses, hotels and youth hostels provides an abundance of opportunities. Nevertheless, after my unfortunate experiences early in the walk, I learnt to have a room booked for the night when I started in the morning and it is a good idea to have reservations for 3-4 nights ahead.

The Tourist Information Centres (TIC) are extremely useful not only for local reservations but also because they can usually help you to 'book a bed ahead'. However, I mostly made reservations myself, using my mobile telephone and the list of accommodation mentioned below. If you walk in the low-season, it is well to remember that not all TICs are open all year round. A list of TICs is available from the British Tourist Authority. Please note that many B&Bs are also closed in the low-season.

Folders with regional information about B&Bs in England are available from the **British Travel Centre, 12 Lower Regent Street, Piccadilly Circus, London SW1Y 4PQ**. Excellent brochures covering various regions in Scotland can be requested from the **Scottish Tourist Board Central Information Department, P.O.Box 705, Edinburgh EH4 3EU (0131 332 2433)**.

There are several good guidebooks giving details about B&B establishments, guest houses and hotels but they are heavy and bulky to carry on the walk. To overcome this problem I cut out details of all interesting places along my planned route, stuck them close together on A4 pages, numbered them and copied everything. This took me a few hours but was time well spent. I left the originals with my family so I could easily communicate my whereabouts by just mentioning a number, and brought the copies with me, only some 8 A4 sheets copied on both sides.

In some areas there may not be any eating places available. Do not forget to ask, when making a B&B reservation, if there are any restaurants within easy walking distance or if an evening meal can be provided at the B&B. If this is not the case, you have been warned and can bring something to stave off hunger.

In the chapter 'Road Directions' I have listed the B&B establishments, guest houses and hotels where I stayed, which may be useful, particularly in the more remote areas. They were generally acceptable, many were good and some were superb, both in terms of comfort and service.

Expenditure

The cost of the journey obviously depends on how many days you spend on the project and the standard you wish to maintain. We can take my journey as an example: I tried to stay in some comfort, but not luxury, and used mostly B&Bs and guest houses, with en suite facilities whenever possible, and the occasional hotel.

The average daily cost for accommodation was £22. It is of course possible to do it more cheaply by staying at less expensive B&Bs, youth hostels etc. For lunch, dinner and snacks I calculated a daily cost of £15-20.

The journey cost me well over £2,000, including maps (about £200), local telephone calls and fares from London to Land's End and from John o' Groats to Edinburgh. (Air tickets to/from Britain are not included). The cost does not include shoes or other equipment you may need to buy. The journey is not inexpensive but it is a once-in-a-lifetime experience.

List of Equipment

As I used a trolley, weight was not a problem. A few pounds extra did not really matter. This is what I packed in the trolley (in a number of plastic bags), apart from the clothes I was wearing (see also 'Clothing'):

Rainwear	Mini flashlight
2 shirts, 1 T-shirt	Telephone + charger
1 sweater	Adapter
4 pairs of socks	Food
2 underpants	Water-bottle (plastic)
Trousers (evening use)	Toothbrush
Extra shoes, boot-wax	Toothpaste
Trainers	Shampoo
Gloves, cap	Deodorant
Spare reading glasses	Foot-balm
Reading matter	Foot-file
Maps	Scissors
Distance meter	Nail-cutter
List of accommodation	Multipurpose knife
List of TICs	Shaver
Camera, film	Plasters
Notebook, pens	Detergent (sachets)
Alarm-clock	Clothes-pegs, Sewing kit

I carried the following items on my person:

Cash	Driving licence
Cheques	Passport
Credit cards	Pedometer
Address/telephone list	Map-case
Insurance papers	Compass

25

Communication

A mobile telephone will make you independent of public or B&B telephones (except in certain areas where reception is poor) and is strongly recommended.

It will be very useful for booking accommodation and also to keep your family informed about your progress. I kept the telephone open for incoming calls on an agreed hour every day. Especially if you are on a solo walk, it is very cheering to receive calls from family and friends.

The telephones are quite small and light. You will of course also have to bring a charger.

How to get to the starting point

South to north: There are trains from London (Paddington) and coaches (Victoria Coach Station) to Penzance. Take a taxi from there to Land's End.

North to south: One alternative is to take the train in Edinburgh over Inverness to Thurso and then a taxi to John o' Groats.

Road Directions

This chapter contains detailed road directions for the route I chose. This route is very direct and includes some major roads. Even if I never felt unsafe, I would perhaps in some instances have chosen alternative and quieter roads if I were to do the walk again. I have often mentioned in the text whether the roads were pleasant or not.

For easy reference I have indicated in bold letters whenever I turned onto a new road and there is a schematic map for each day's walk. Do your own homework but perhaps my route may be of some help.

Information is provided regarding which Landranger maps to use on the respective days and I have also mentioned the places where I spent the nights.

There is a wealth of beautiful and interesting places to visit in Britain but I have made very few references to such places. You will stumble upon many of them as you go along but a good idea is, again, to do some homework and have a list of places you wish to see and things you wish to do.

Key (to all maps):

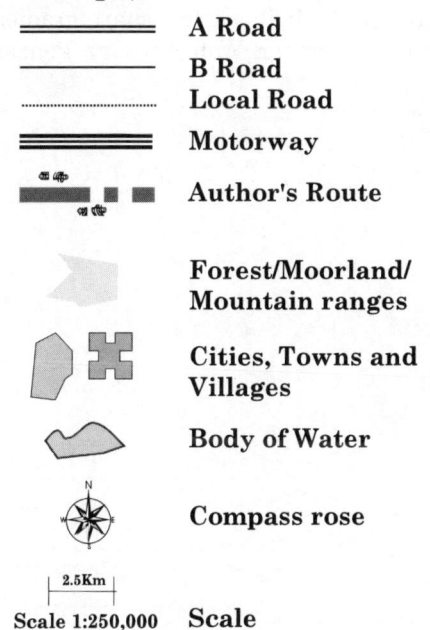

A Road

B Road

Local Road

Motorway

Author's Route

Forest/Moorland/
Mountain ranges

Cities, Towns and
Villages

Body of Water

Compass rose

2.5Km

Scale 1:250,000   Scale

27

Map: Landranger 203

The night before the start of the walk is most conveniently spent at the excellent Land's End Hotel (01736 871501) where there is interesting information about the 'End to End' journey. In the morning walk the few steps to the First and Last House and perhaps to the cliffs below where you can, for a while, be the most south-westerly human being on the British mainland.

As I walked in the low-season I used the **A30,** which was rather quiet, for the first 10 miles to Penzance but at other times it is preferable to turn right after about ½ mile onto the B3315 which is quieter and more scenic. It has a few sharp gradients and is also somewhat longer. Walk through Penzance and rejoin

Land's
End

the **A30**. Before Hayle turn onto the **B3301** through Hayle and take a **local road** to Connor Downs, where I stayed at the peaceful Eureka Villa, 34, Turnpike Road (0736 754105).

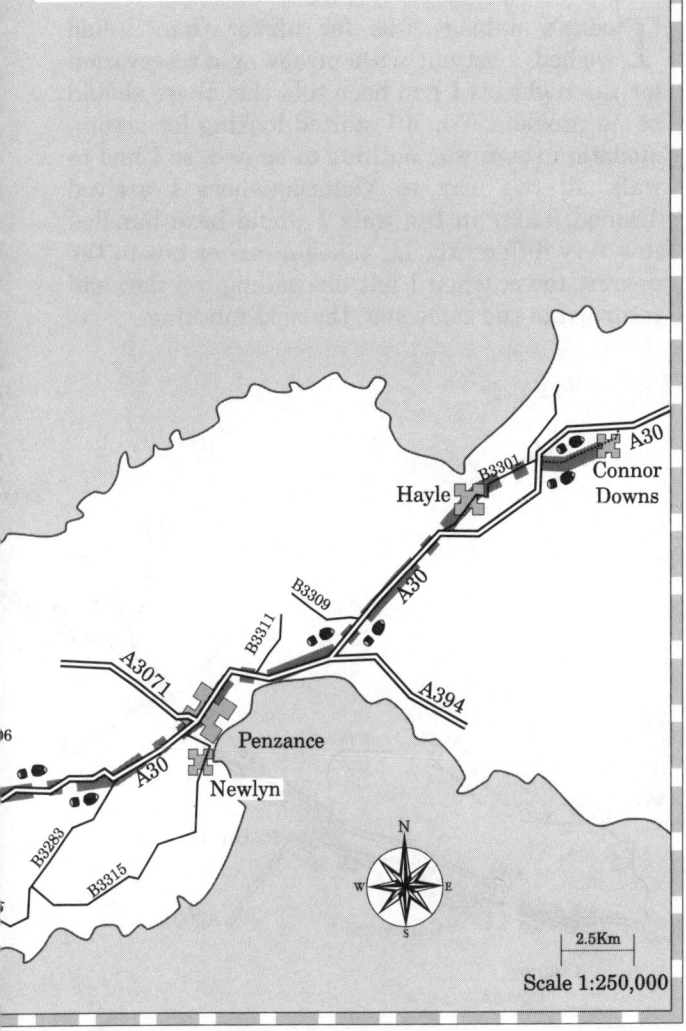

DAY 2.
CONNOR DOWNS – VICTORIA
31 MILES – 50 KM

Maps: Landranger 203, 204, 200

Today's mileage was far higher than I had wished. I set out without having a reservation for the night, as I had been told that there should be no problem. When I started looking for accommodation there was nothing to be had, so I had to walk all the way to Victoria where I arrived drained. Later in the walk I would have handled this very differently, i.e. taken a taxi or bus to the nearest town, when I felt like calling it a day, and returned to the same spot the next morning.

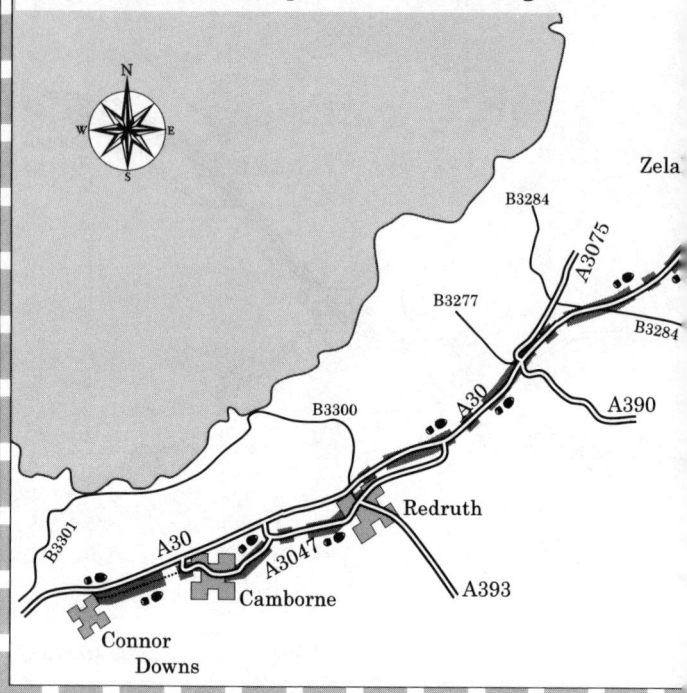

Continue on the **local road** and take the **A3047** through Camborne and rejoin the **A30** in Redruth. To get some relief from this busy stretch of the A30 turn off onto a **local road** in Mitchell to Indian Queens and again the **A30** to Victoria, where I was resuscitated at Victoria Guest House (0726 890 316), a very friendly and family-run establishment.

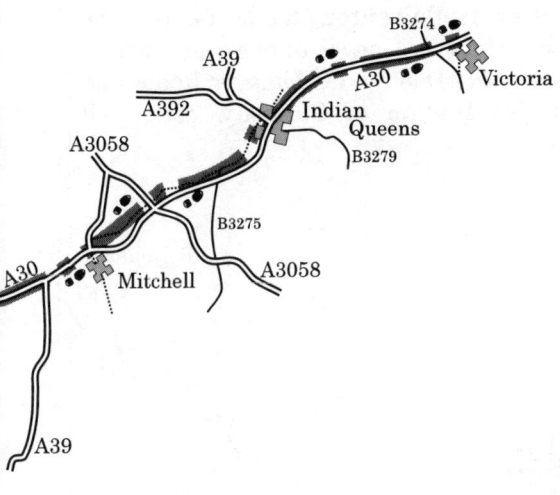

DAY 3.
VICTORIA – BOLVENTOR
17 MILES – 27 KM

Maps: Landranger 200, 201

A brief spell on the **A30** before turning left onto a **local road** over Lamorick and the **A389** through Bodmin and a **local road** back onto the **A30** to Bolventor. I chose this route (there are alternative minor roads) because I wanted to stay at the classic, and very comfortable, Jamaica Inn (01566 86250), Bolventor, made famous by Daphne du Maurier's novel of the same name. There is a Dame Daphne du Maurier Room and Mr. Potter's Museum of Curiosity, both well worth a visit.

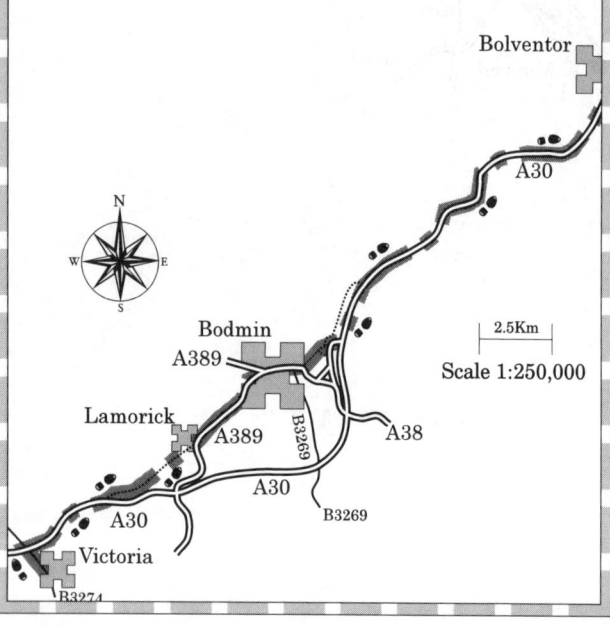

DAY 4.
BOLVENTOR – LIFTON
16 MILES – 26 KM

Map: Landranger 201

The **A30** again but take the **local road** near Altarnun which soon rejoins the **A30**. After Launceston you leave Cornwall behind and enter Devon. This feels as if the first chapter has been completed. At Liftondown take a **local road** (which is the old A30) to the pleasant village of Lifton and the quiet Mayfield Guest House (01566 784401), at the far end of the village.

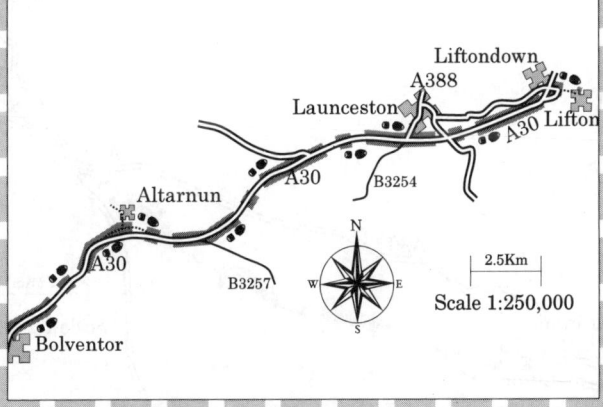

DAY 5.
LIFTON – CREDITON
33 MILES – 53 KM

Maps: Landranger 201, 191

Again I innocently trusted local information – I would easily find accommodation after Okehampton. There were neither B&B signs nor hotels in sight when I started to look. The kind staff at the Countryman's Inn made some ten tele-

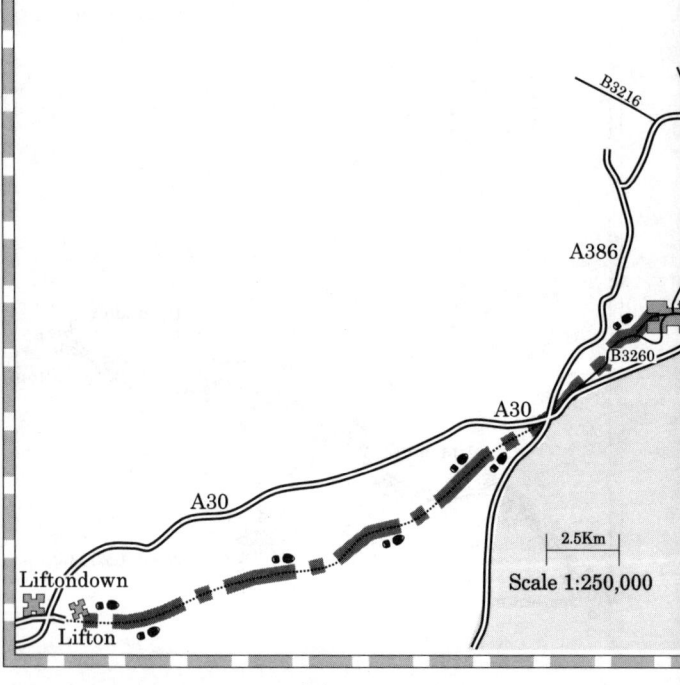

phone calls but could not find me a bed for the night. In the end I had to speedwalk to Crediton, where I finally found a delightful and comfortable place, Libbetts Cottage, Church Street (01363 772709). Do ask your hostess to make some pancakes for your breakfast. They are delicious.

The roads: Continue on the **local road** and take the **B3260** to Okehampton. Then the **B3215**, the **A3072**, and the **A377** to Crediton. A nice walk but far too long, for me at least.

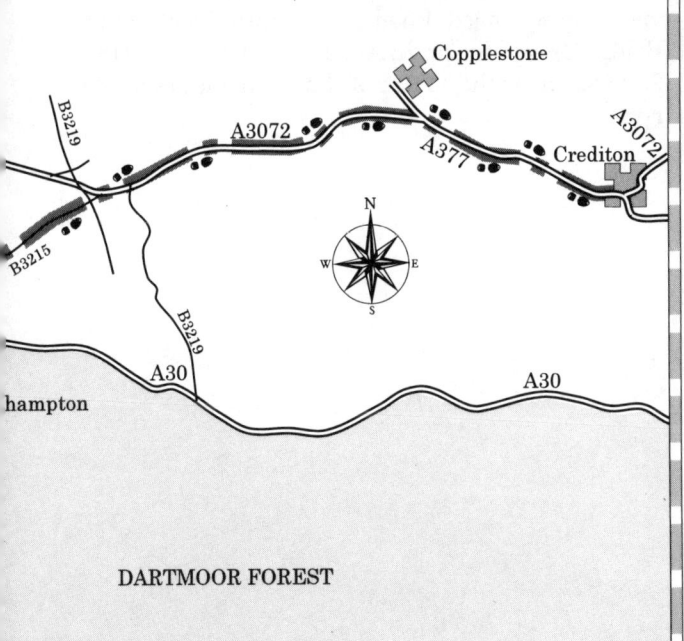

DAY 6.
CREDITON – TIVERTON
12 MILES – 19 KM

Maps: Landranger 191, 192, 181

Leave Crediton on the **A3072** and walk to Bickleigh. The road offers some ascents and descents, but nothing too taxing, and the countryside is lovely. Bickleigh, on the River Exe, is a delightful little village with several hotels and restaurants. I wish I had encountered such a place halfway yesterday.

From Bickleigh take the **A396** to Tiverton. The Exe will accompany you all the way, on your right. Tiverton is a pleasant market town with all the services you will need. I had booked into the attractive Bridge Guest House, 23 Angel Hill, Tiverton (01884 252804), near the centre of the town and beside the river.

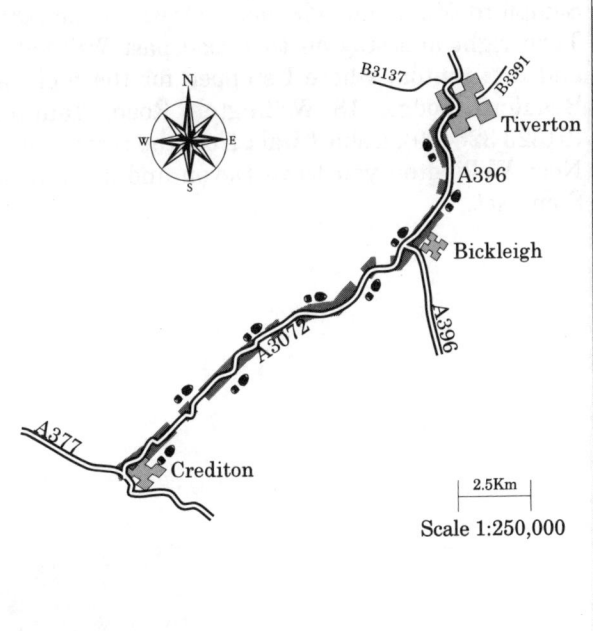

B3137

B3391

Tiverton

A396

Bickleigh

A396

A3072

A377

Crediton

2.5Km

Scale 1:250,000

DAY 7.
TIVERTON – TAUNTON
22 MILES – 35 KM

Maps: 181, 193

Take the **B3391** and after ½ mile or so turn right onto a **local road** across the A361 to Bradford and over Whitnage, Westleigh and Burlescombe, where there is a stiff ascent, to the **A38.** Turn left and after a couple of hundred yards right onto a **local road**, running parallel with the M5, over Sampford Moor and Pleamore Cross to the **A38.** Turn right and stay on this road past Wellington and to Taunton, where I stopped for the night at Beauford Lodge, 18 Wellington Road, Taunton (01823 326420), a short walk from the town centre. Near Wellington you leave Devon and are now in Somerset.

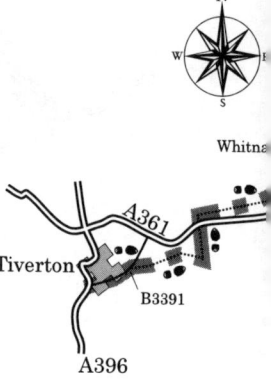

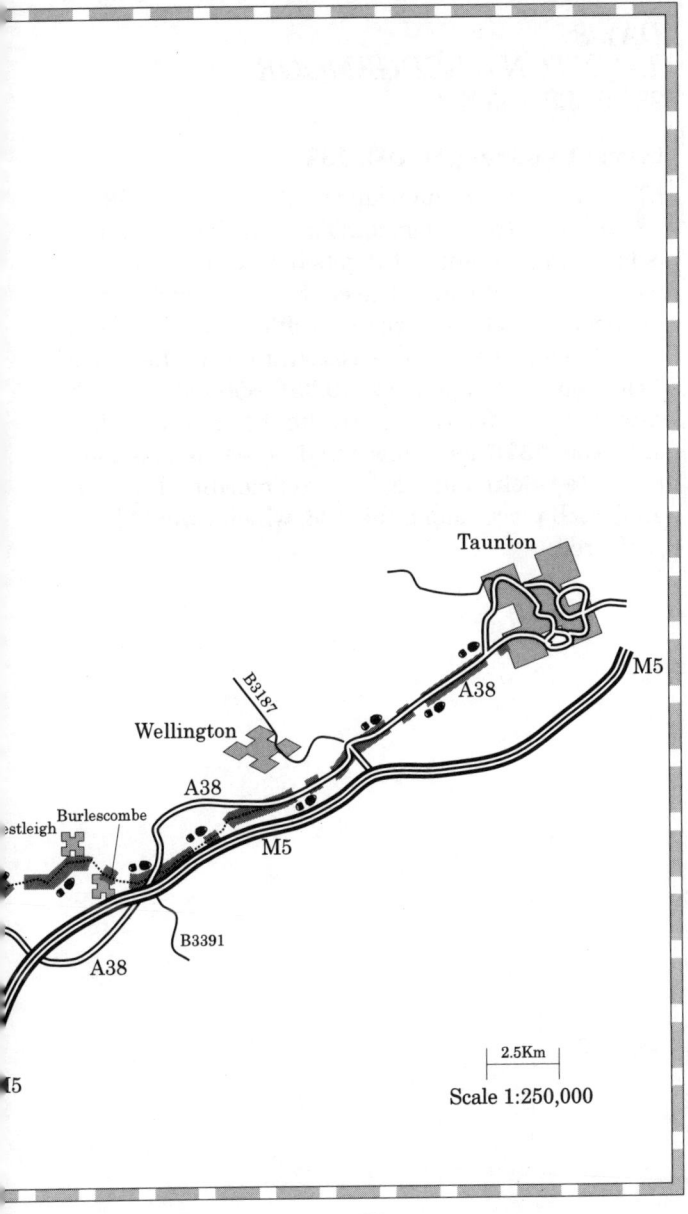

Taunton

M5

B3187

A38

Wellington

A38

Burlescombe

estleigh

M5

B3391

A38

5

2.5Km

Scale 1:250,000

Maps: Landranger 193, 182

Today's navigation is uncomplicated, the **A38** all the way to Sedgemoor. The exit from Taunton is fairly unpleasant but it gets better after the road where the local traffic leaves the M5. From a great distance the characteristic profile of Brent Knoll can be seen. As I had a reservation at the Forte Travelodge, Sedgemoor (0800 850950), which caters mainly for the M5 traffic, I had to turn left onto the **A370** for a few hundred yards and then navigate **backroads**. Early next morning I discovered B&B places along the A38, which I would have preferred.

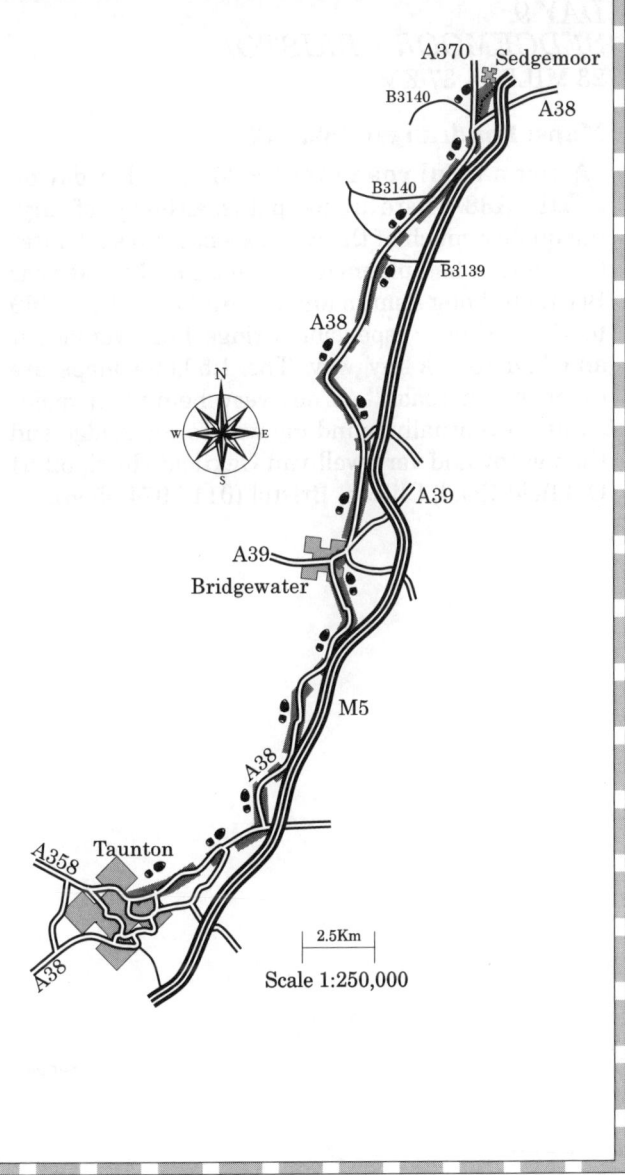

A370
Sedgemoor
B3140
A38
B3140
B3139
A38
N
W E
S
A39
A39
Bridgewater
M5
A38
A358
Taunton
A38

2.5Km
Scale 1:250,000

41

DAY 9.
SEDGEMOOR – BRISTOL
23 MILES – 37 KM

Maps: Landranger 182, 172

After a **local road** over the M5 another day on the **A38**. There are footpaths, although of varying quality, much of the way, except for a spell after Churchill. I had planned to take a **local road** near Bristol to Long Ashton and the **A370** and the **A369** to the Clifton Suspension Bridge but overshot it and had to ask my way. The 1:50,000 maps are excellent on roads but not very helpful in major cities. I eventually found my way to the bridge and the nearby and very well-run Oakfield Hotel, 52-54 Oakfield Road, Clifton, Bristol (0117 974 5556).

Sedgemoor

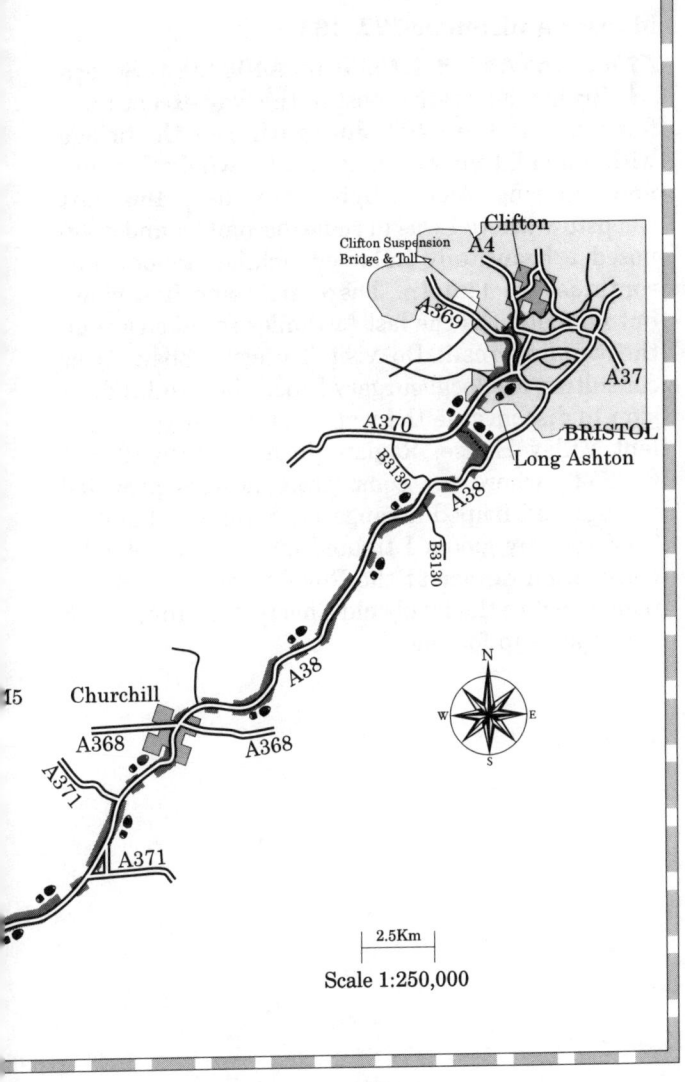

Clifton

Clifton Suspension
Bridge & Toll

A4

A369

A37

A370

BRISTOL

Long Ashton

B3130

A38

B3130

A38

15

Churchill

A368

A368

A371

A371

N
W E
S

2.5Km
Scale 1:250,000

DAY 10.
BRISTOL – TINTERN
23 MILES – 37 KM

Maps: Landranger 172, 162

Take the **A4018**, **B4055** and **A403** to the Severn Bridge. Footpaths most of the way except for a few miles on the A403. **Footpath** over the bridge with splendid views but it can be windy. You are now entering Wales. Right onto the **A466** past Chepstow where I was in some discomfort and diagnosed a beautifully inflamed Achilles tendon but continued to Tintern. There are some fine views but no footpaths the last few miles so take care on the winding road. Do visit Tintern Abbey. After consulting the local surgery I took the painful decision to discontinue the walk. I stayed at the excellent Valley House, Raglan Road, Tintern (01291 689652), where my considerate hostess provided icebags and helped arrange my return to London. To dispel my gloom I treated myself to a splendid consolation dinner at the Royal George Hotel and paid a visit to the lovely old Cherry Tree Inn, which was, sadly, up for sale.

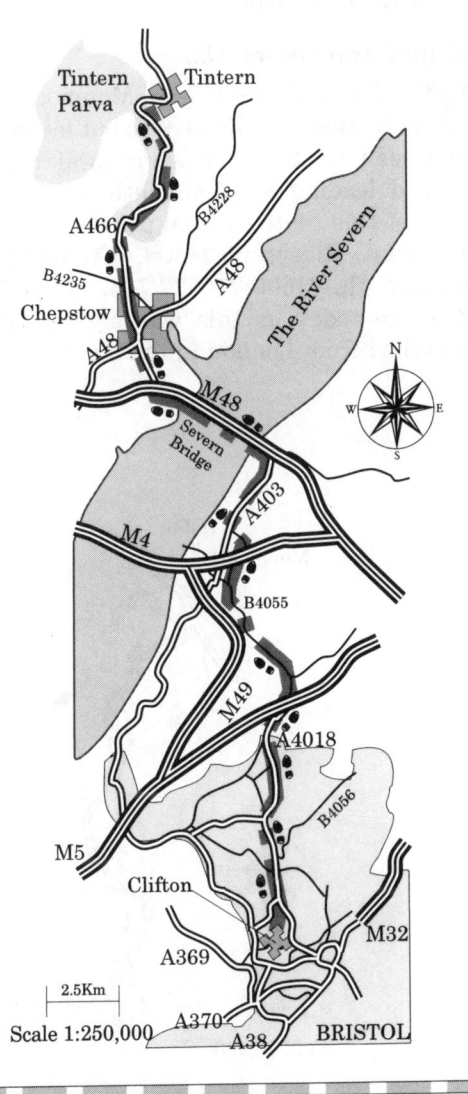

Tintern Parva

Tintern

B4228

A466

The River Severn

B4235

Chepstow

A48

A48

M48

Severn Bridge

A403

M4

B4055

M49

A4018

B4056

M5

Clifton

A4018

M32

A369

2.5Km

Scale 1:250,000

A370

A38

BRISTOL

N
W   E
S

DAY 11.
TINTERN – MONMOUTH
11 MILES – 18 KM

Map: Landranger 162

The **A466** all the way to Monmouth. A lovely walk along the River Wye but few footpaths. I had seen on the map some local roads and a B-road leading to Monmouth but was advised against this route by local people. I stayed at the excellent Riverside Hotel, Cinderhill Street, Monmouth (01600 715577/713236). Only a short distance today as this was my restart, having travelled from London in the morning.

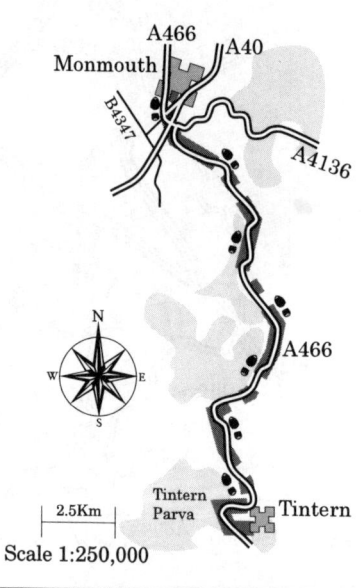

DAY 12.
MONMOUTH – HEREFORD
18 MILES – 29 KM

Maps: Landranger 162, 149

Continue on the **A466** through pleasant landscape. There are few footpaths but the road should not be dangerous to the careful walker. There are few eating places en route but in Wormelow Tump, where the A466 and the B4348 meet, there is a Post Office-cum-shop or you can have a sitdown meal at the nearby Tump Inn. Turn left onto the **A49** into Hereford. This stretch is bad for walking, no footpaths and no hard shoulders, but it is a short distance. If you do not mind a detour, there are alternative local roads. My comfortable B&B in Hereford was the Charades, 34 Southbank Road (01432 269444).

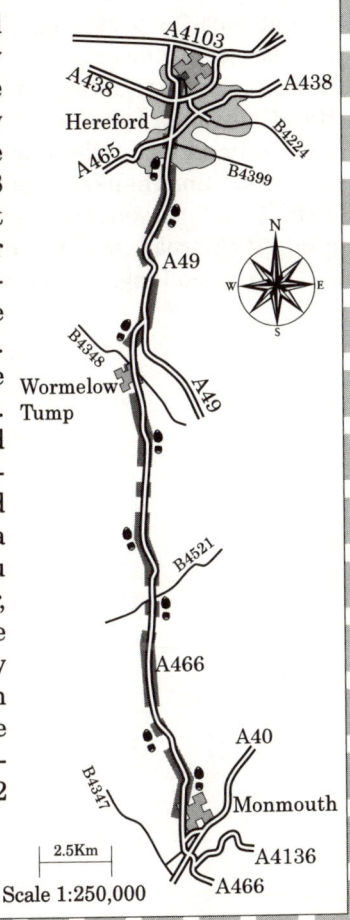

A4103

A438   A438

Hereford   B4224

A465   B4399

A49

B4348

Wormelow   A49
Tump

B4521

A466

A40

B4347   Monmouth

2.5Km   A4136

Scale 1:250,000   A466

47

DAY 13.
HEREFORD – RICHARDS CASTLE
21 MILES – 34 KM

Maps: Landranger 149, 138

Depart from Hereford on the **A49** which, at first, is equally bad going north. There are dual carriageways with hard shoulders after Wellington, though not for very long. The landscape is fairly flat except at Queens Wood where there is a very long, but not a too steep ascent. Turn left onto the **B4361** through Leominster, a good place for lunch, and to Richards Castle where I stayed in a pleasant room at Longbanks, Woodhouse Lane (01584 831636), a farmhouse set in rural landscape. This is a bit off the road, so ask your hosts to pick you up.

There is no longer a castle in Richards Castle!

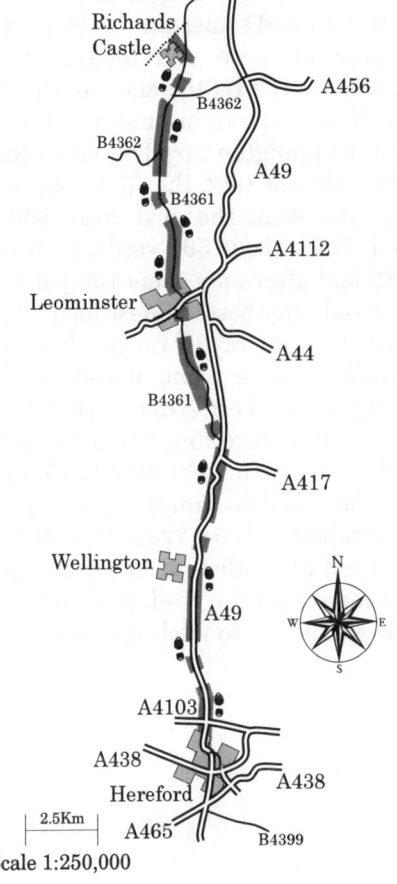

Richards
Castle

A456

B4362

B4362

A49

B4361

A4112

Leominster

A44

B4361

A417

Wellington

A49

A4103

A438

A438

Hereford

A465

B4399

| 2.5Km
Scale 1:250,000

49

Map: Landranger 138

Continue on the **B4361**. There is soon a footpath all the way into the delightful town of Ludlow. Buy sandwiches and something to drink, as there is nothing between here and today's destination. Leave Ludlow on the **B4361** and join the **A49** for ½ mile or so. Then turn right onto the **B4365**. About a mile after Culmington turn left onto a **local road** to New Ho. *Do not* take the first road which is a cul-de-sac. You want the next road, which is not signposted. Walk about 500 yards, turn right onto the **B4368** and after only some 100 yards left onto a **local road** signposted Westhope, Ticklerton. Then thread your way through these places to Hope Bowdler. These tranquil country lanes are roadwalking at its best. Now turn left onto the **B4371** to Church Stretton. Cross the **A49** at the traffic lights and turn right onto the **B4370** to All Stretton. The excellent Jinley Guest House, Castle Hill, All Stretton (01694 723243), which enjoys a scenic location and offers good service, is about a strenuous mile from the road, so if you are staying there, ask your hosts to fetch you by car.

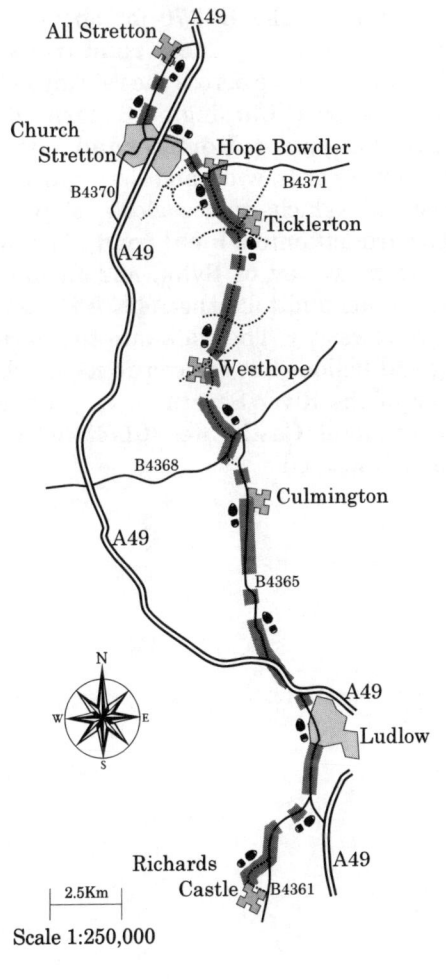

All Stretton

A49

Church
Stretton

Hope Bowdler

B4370

B4371

A49

Ticklerton

Westhope

B4368

Culmington

A49

B4365

A49

Ludlow

N
W E
S

A49

Richards
Castle

B4361

2.5Km

Scale 1:250,000

Maps: Landranger 138, 126

Continue on the **B4370** for about ½ mile and turn right onto a **local road** (not signposted) and another ½ mile across the railway and the **A49**. At the signpost 'Cardington 3' turn left onto the straight but narrow **Roman road,** often not more than three yards wide and very quiet. When the occasional vehicle comes along, step well to the side. Turn left onto a **local road** after Green Farm and walk by way of Ryton and Condover (lovely walk so far) and take the **A49, A5112** and **A5197** into Shrewsbury. The walk into the town centre is long and tedious but the centre itself, which lies in a loop of the River Severn, is very attractive. The Lucroft Hotel, Castlegates (01743 362421), is conveniently located.

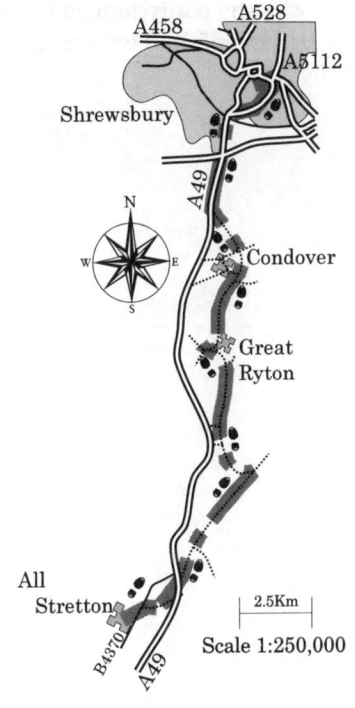

A458

A528

A5112

Shrewsbury

N
W E
S

A49

Condover

Great
Ryton

All
Stretton

B4370

A49

2.5Km

Scale 1:250,000

DAY 16.
SHREWSBURY – WHITCHURCH
21 MILES – 34 KM

Maps: Landranger 126, 117

Take the **A528** out of Shrewsbury. The footpath stops after a couple of miles. At Harmer Hill turn onto the **B5476** all the way to Whitchurch. Supplies and food can be had in Wem. Rather flat landscape today. Not unpleasant but it gets monotonous after a while. My peaceful B&B in Whitchurch was the oddly named Chemistry Farm, Chemistry (01948 665263) with canal boats moving tranquilly by.

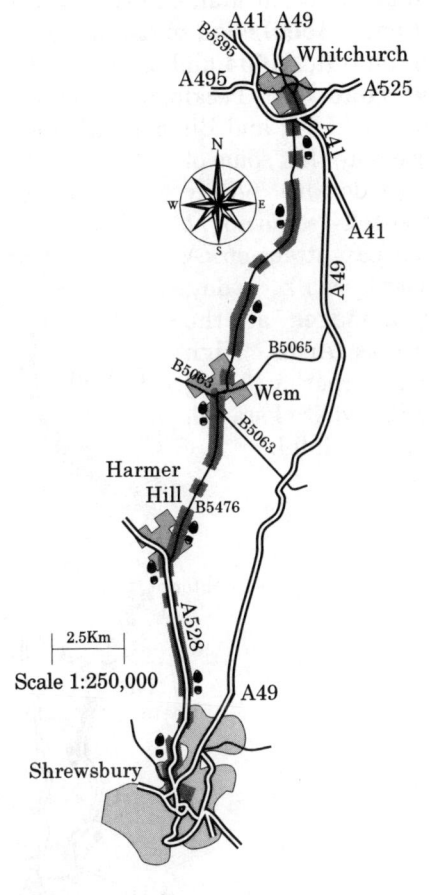

A41 A49
B5395
Whitchurch
A495
A525
A41
A41
A49
N
W E
S
B5065
B5064
Wem
B5063
Harmer
Hill
B5476
2.5Km
A528
Scale 1:250,000
A49
Shrewsbury

DAY 17.
WHITCHURCH – TARPORLEY
16 MILES – 26 KM

Map: Landranger 117

The **A41** towards Chester. Footpath of varying quality to No Man's Heath where you turn right onto a **local road** to Ashtons cross and right again onto the **A534** and after ½ mile left onto a **local road** over Peckforton, the Castle Farm, Wharton's Lock and Birch Heath into Tarporley.

Please note that some of the roads are poorly signposted – some not at all, so pay attention. A pleasant walk today. The manager at the Foresters Arms, High Street, Tarporley (01829 733151), where I stayed, was very helpful.

A49
Tarporley
A51
A49
Peckforton
A534
A534
Ashtons Cross
A49
No Man's Heath
N
W E
S
A41
Whitchurch

2.5Km

Scale 1:250,000

DAY 18.
TARPORLEY – RUNCORN
17 MILES – 27 KM

Maps: Landranger 117, 108

On your way out of Tarporley turn right onto a **local road** to the **A49**. At Cotebrook turn left onto the **B5152** to Frodsham. This road is pleasant, especially through Delamere Forest, where there are picnic sites. There are a couple of pubs and places to buy snacks. In Frodsham turn right onto the **A56**, cross the bridge and bear left onto the **A557** into Runcorn. Study your maps carefully. It is easy to get lost. At least I did, but finally reached the modern Campanile Hotel, Lowlands Road, Runcorn (01928 581771), near the railway station and the Old Town. There is an excellent restaurant at the hotel.

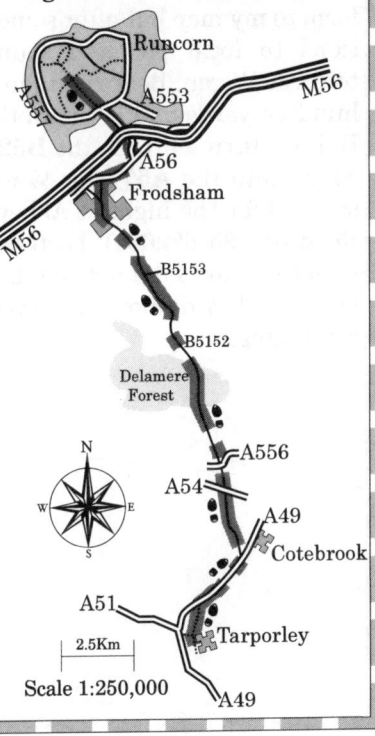

DAY 19.
RUNCORN – ORRELL
16 MILES – 26 KM

Map: Landranger 108

Take the **A533** over the very busy Runcorn-Widnes Bridge, using the footpath on the right side. Then a **local road** through an industrial area to the **A568**. This is a rather miserable start to the morning but it gets somewhat better later. Then the **A569** and **A570**. The A569 was closed to motorised traffic and not signposted, but walkers can get through.

Near St Helens the road numbers did not conform to my map but after some confusion and questions to local people I found the **A571** north towards Wigan. Bear right onto the **A580** for a few hundred yards and left onto the **A571** again. After Billinge turn left onto the **B5206** to Orrell and left again onto the **A577** for ½ mile or so to where I stopped for the night at Abbey Lakes Hotel, Orrell Road (01695 622664), hostessed by a former Miss Great Britain. I did not spot her, though. There is a pub but they do not serve evening meals, so bring something.

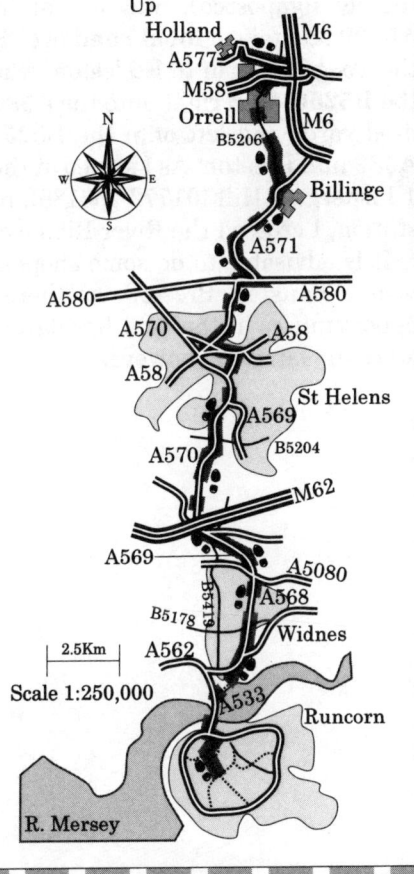

Maps: Landranger 108, 102

Continue on the **A577** for about a mile to where the road makes a very sharp bend (there is a monument on the left) and turn onto a **local road** north to Appley Bridge and left onto the **B5375** (poorly signposted). Stay on this road across the **A5209** and take a **local road** over Robin Hood and the Toogood Farm to Eccleston, where you pick up the **B5250**, turn right onto the **A581** for a few hundred yards and left onto the **B5253** and then the **A582** into Preston. As I stayed at the County Hotel, 1 Fishergate Hill (01772 253188), near the railway station, I crossed the River Ribble on the **A59**.

It is advisable to do some shopping and perhaps visit a bank in Preston, as there are not many opportunities in the next few days. There is a food store in Garstang, however.

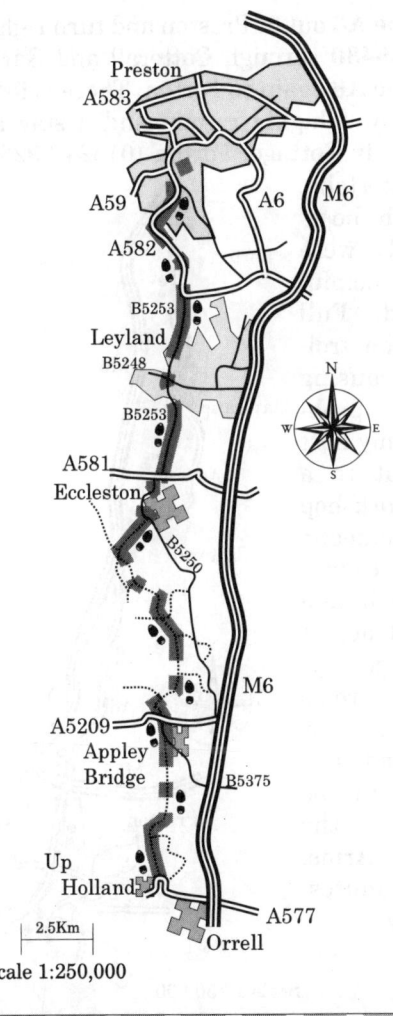

Preston
A583

A59   A6   M6

A582

B5253

Leyland

B5248

B5253

A581
Eccleston

B5250

M6

A5209
Appley
Bridge

B5375

Up
Holland

A577

Orrell

2.5Km

Scale 1:250,000

DAY 21.
PRESTON – FORTON
14 MILES – 23 KM

Map: Landranger 102

Take the **A6** out of Preston and turn right onto the **B6430** through Catterall and Garstang. Pick up the **A6** again to Forton. There is footpath all the way. I highly recommend a stay at the Middle Holly Cottage, Forton (01524 792399), a most comfortable place with hosts who really were extremely helpful and kind. Full marks! The trolley was causing me some problems and my host brought it to a nearby workshop where someone did an excellent welding job and would not accept payment, justifying the area's reputation for hospitality. Dinner can be had at the Hamilton Arms, a few minutes' walk away.

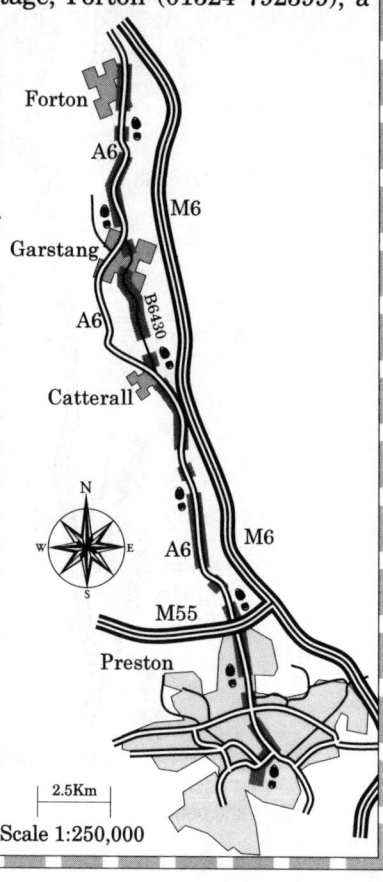

DAY 22.
FORTON – KIRKBY LONSDALE
24 MILES – 39 KM

Maps: Landranger 102, 97

Continue on the **A6** for about two miles and turn right onto a **local road** at Bay Horse, signposted Quernmore 6. Walk by way of Quernmore to Caton. This is a beautiful and quiet walk. Turn right onto a **local road** through Brookhouse to the **A683**. Turn right here and left onto the **A65** and

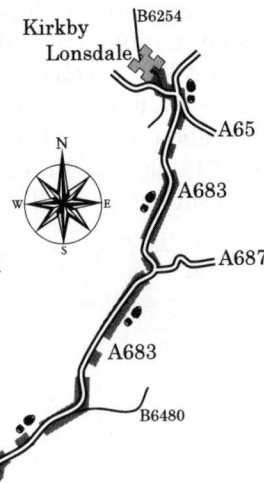

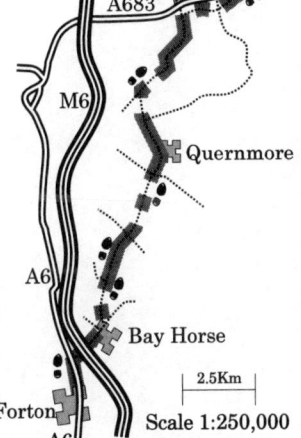

right onto the **B6254** into Kirkby Lonsdale, an attractive little town, where I had booked into the Copper Kettle, Market Street (01524 271714) a small restaurant with some rooms upstairs. Do take in Ruskin's view, a famous beauty spot.

Maps: Landranger 97, 91

Take the **A683** north from Kirkby Lonsdale and bear left onto the **B6256**, right onto the **A684** for about ½ mile, left onto the **B6257**, and right onto the **A685** to Tebay.

A lovely walk today with splendid views but also some gradients. I checked into The Cross Keys Inn, Tebay (015396 24240), in the centre of the village, where a satisfying meal can be had.

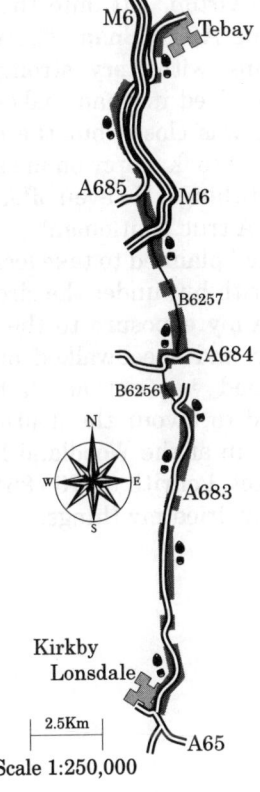

M6

Tebay

A685

M6

B6257

A684

B6256

N

W E

S

A683

Kirkby
Lonsdale

2.5Km

A65

Scale 1:250,000

Maps: Landranger 91, 90

The **B6260** to Orton, left onto the **B6261** and right onto the **A6** to Shap. The weather this day was appalling with very strong winds and heavy rain so I arrived in Shap soaked and miserable. Everything was closed but the proprietor of the Greyhound Inn took mercy on me and let me in to change my wet things. He even offered me a welcome cup of tea. A true gentleman!

From Shap I had planned to take local roads over Bampton to Penrith but under the circumstances I decided to make my exposure to the elements as brief as possible and speedwalked on the **A6** to Penrith. This road was not at all busy, as the motorists seemed to favour the nearby M6. I was grateful to check in at the Woodland House Hotel, Wordsworth Street, Penrith (01768 864177), where the hostess kindly dried my things.

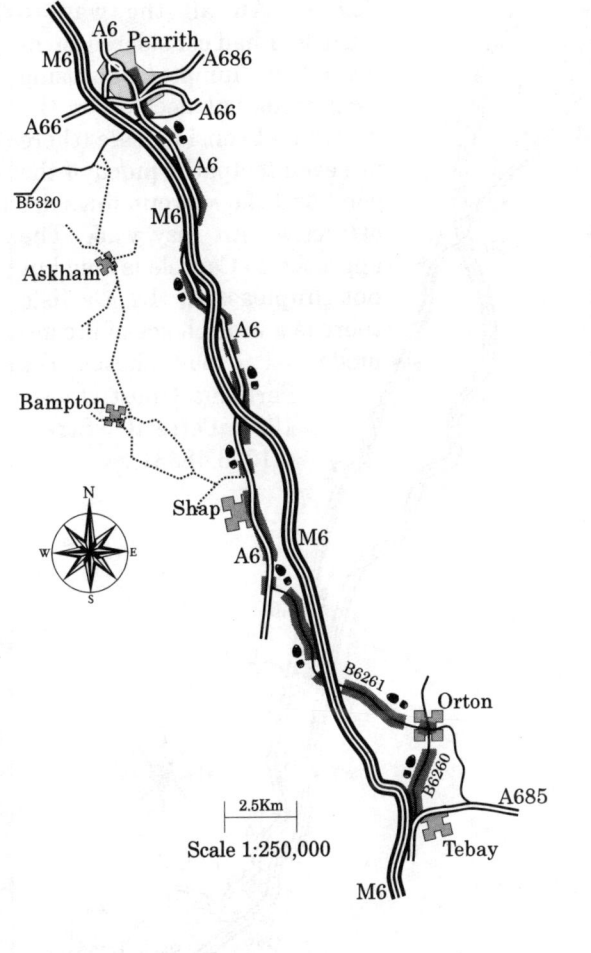

Maps: Landranger 90, 85

Easy map-reading today: The **A6** all the way to Carlisle. I had considered turning left in Plumpton and using local roads but decided on the A6 which I consider safe (there are even footpaths much of the way) and the surroundings are attractive. An easy walk. The approach to Carlisle is long but not unpleasant. In Carlisle there is a wide choice of accommodation. I had chosen the Parkland Guest House, 136 Petteril Street (01228 48331).

68

DAY 26.
CARLISLE – EAGLESFIELD
24 MILES – 39 KM

Map: Landranger 85

Bring a packed lunch since there are few opportunities to buy food today. The A74 north of Carlisle now has motorway status and is out of bounds to pedestrians, which will cost you an hour or so extra. Take the **A7** out of Carlisle to Longtown. Cross the River Esk and turn left onto the **A6071** and right onto a **local road** to Springfield where you will cross the border to Scotland, a major milestone. Continue on the **B7076**, over Kirkpatrick Fleming, until you turn right onto a **local road**, signposted 'Eaglesfield' and crossing the motorway. Today's walk has been over quite flat and rather uninspiring terrain. I stayed at

the very pleasant farmhouse Glengower (01461 500253), a mile or so from the village.

DAY 27.
EAGLESFIELD – BORELAND
12 MILES – 19 KM

Maps: Landranger 85, 79

Today's walk will be short because the choice of accommodation is very limited. So are eating places. In fact, there is nothing at all, so be prepared. In Eaglesfield turn onto the **B722** to Waterbeck and, there, left after the church onto a **local road** signposted 'Corrie'. Left onto the **B7068** and a **local road** over Corrie Common to Boreland where you will meet the **B723**. A lovely walk in a sparsely populated countryside. I found a very good and friendly B&B in Boreland, the Nether Boreland Farm (01576 610248).

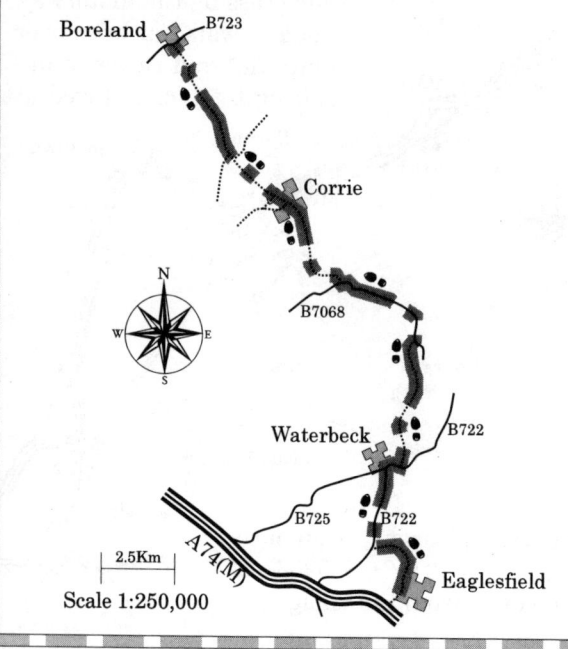

DAY 28.
BORELAND – MOFFAT
12 MILES – 19 KM

Maps: Landranger 79, 78

Another short walk for the same reason as the previous day. You should be in Moffat in time for lunch. Take the **B723** across the river and turn right onto a **local road** over Gillesbie and Pumplaburn and left onto the **A708** into Moffat. I spent the night at the pleasant and centrally located Seamore House, Academy Road, Moffat (01683 220404).

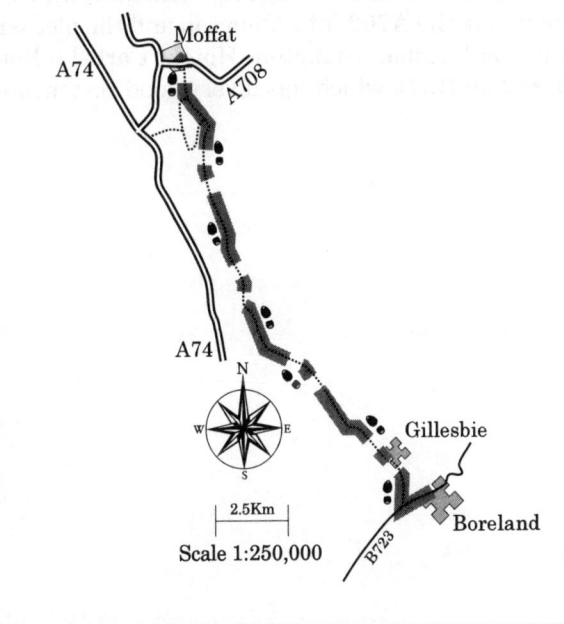

Scale 1:250,000

2.5Km

Maps: Landranger 78, 72

Bring food and drink. The day will start with a very long gradual ascent soon followed by a corresponding descent. Take the **A701** north from Moffat and turn left onto the **B719** to the **A74**. A pleasant walk so far but the dual carriageway A74, which here did not have motorway status, is a busy and fast road. There is a hard shoulder all the way but for a few miles it is very narrow. Walk carefully. After about 5 miles the motorway begins and you must turn left onto the **B7076**. Assuming that you have been walking on the right-hand carriageway, which you should, cross the road with extreme care. Then take the **A702** into Abington and the pleasant and comfortable Abington Hotel, Carlisle Road (01864 502467), which has a very good restaurant.

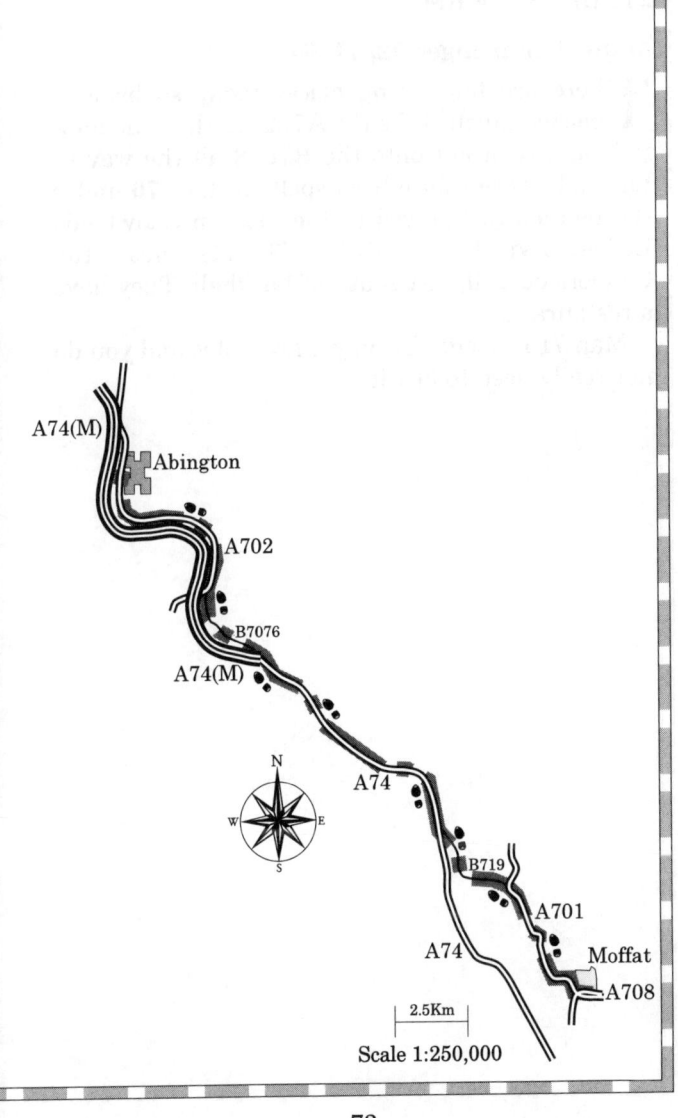

A74(M)

Abington

A702

B7076

A74(M)

A74

B719

A701

Moffat

A74

A708

N
W E
S

2.5Km

Scale 1:250,000

DAY 30.
ABINGTON – LARKHALL
21 MILES – 34 KM

Maps: Landranger 72, 71, 64

There are few eating places today so bring a packed lunch. Take the **A702** north for about a mile and turn left onto the **B7078** all the way to Larkhall, except for a brief spell on the **A70** under the motorway. I stayed at the modern Shawlands Lodge, Ayr Road (01698 791111), near the Canderside Toll, just south of Larkhall. They have a restaurant.

Map 71 is useful for only a few miles and you do not really need to buy it.

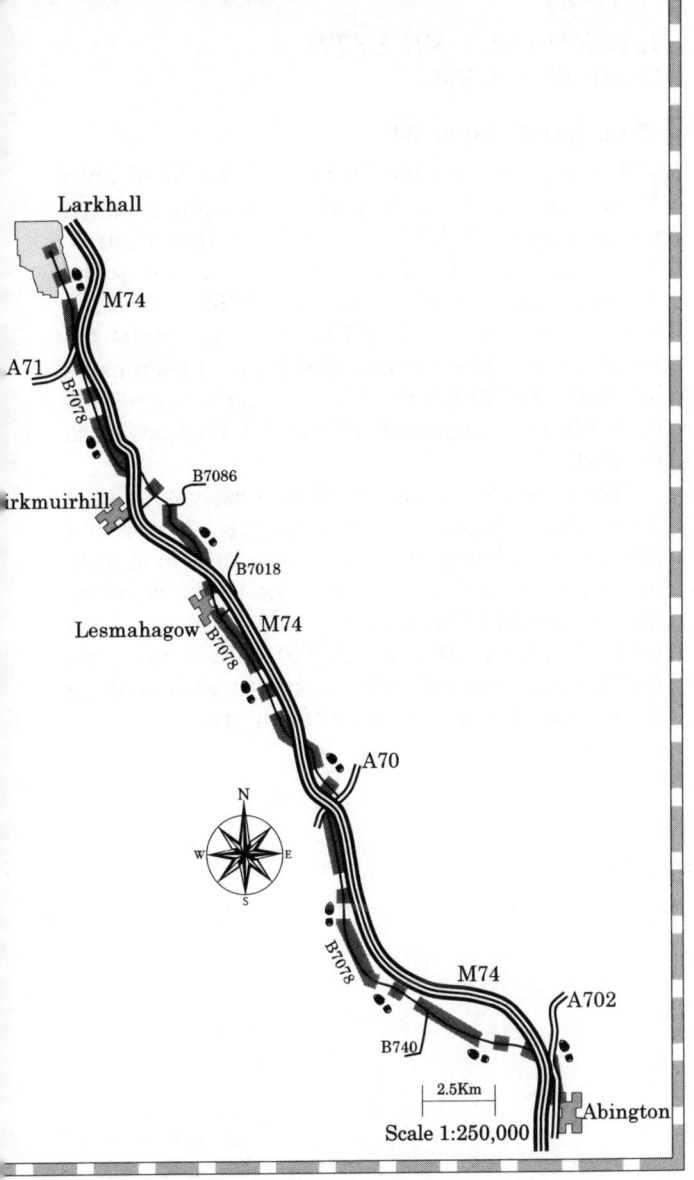

Larkhall

M74

A71

B7078

irkmuirhill

B7086

B7018

Lesmahagow

B7078

M74

A70

N

W E

S

B7078

M74

A702

B740

2.5Km

Scale 1:250,000

Abington

Map: Landranger 64

Continue on the **B7078** through Larkhall onto the **A72** to Hamilton. Carry straight on until you pick up the **B7071**, going past the Race Course. Turn right onto the **A725** and, after crossing the railway, turn right onto the **B7070** through Bellshill and rejoin the **A725.** Then the **B804** for about a mile, right onto the **B803** and at Glenmavis left onto the **B802** into Kilsyth. The latter road is probably not signposted, at least I did not see it, so be alert.

Today's walk is through fairly densely populated areas, but I found it surprisingly nice. A long and steep ascent, not welcome at the end of a long walk (ask to be picked up), brought me to the comfortable Allanfauld Farm, Allanfauld, in the northern part of Kilsyth (01236 822155), where my kind hostess provided valuable assistance with booking accommodation ahead in a difficult area.

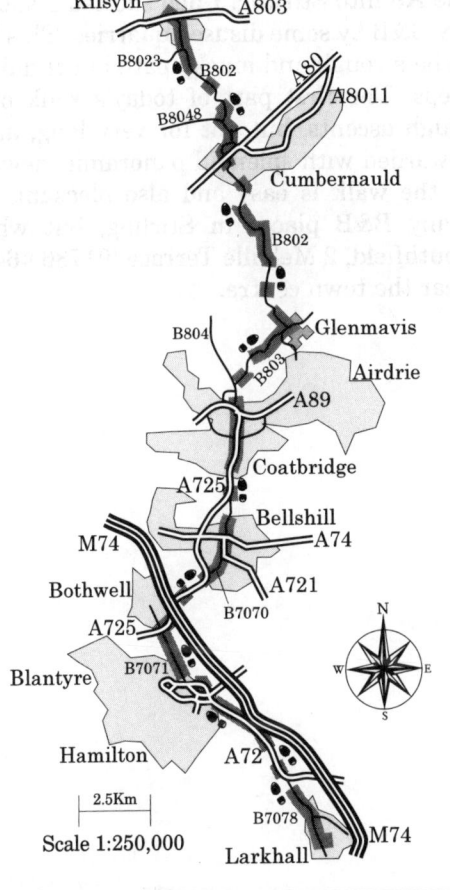

DAY 32.
KILSYTH – STIRLING
13 MILES – 21 KM

Maps: Landranger 64, 57

A short walk to allow for some rest, shopping etc. in pleasant Stirling. Take a **local road** from Kilsyth over Carron Bridge and via the **A872** and the **A9** into Stirling. I had spotted a shortcut from my B&B by some disused quarries. This turned out to be a rough and mucky path but it did save some steps. The first part of today's walk offers some tough ascents, but not for very long, and you are rewarded with splendid panoramic views. The rest of the walk is easy and also pleasant. There are many B&B places in Stirling, but why not try Southfield, 2 Melville Terrace (01786 464872), very near the town centre.

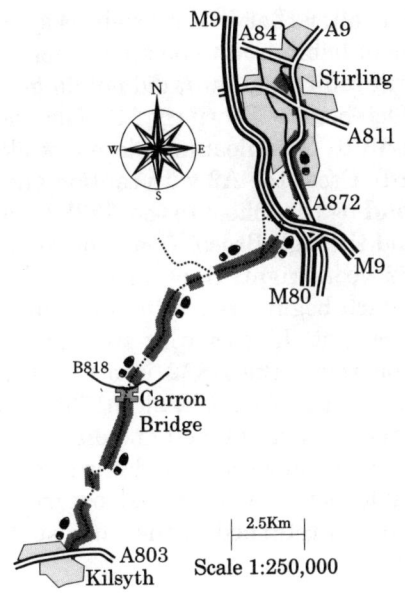

M9
A84
A9
Stirling
A811
A872
M9
M80
B818
Carron
Bridge
A803
Kilsyth

2.5Km
Scale 1:250,000

DAY 33.
STIRLING – CRIEFF
20 MILES – 32 KM

Maps: Landranger 57, 58

Take the **A9** north out of Stirling and the **B998** past the Wallace Monument. Just before reaching the A91 turn left at the church onto a **local road**. This road starts with a long and rather stiff ascent but after that it is a lovely, easy walk with few signs of habitation to be seen. There is an inn, the Sheriff Muir Inn, but it did not do me any good (closed October 7 – February 24). Turn left onto a **local road** to Greenloaning (do not walk towards Blackford). Cross the **A9** with caution and take the **local road** by the school to the **A822** (Old Military Road) and through Braco. A mile or so after Braco the A822 veers right. Stay on the **Old Military Road**, which begins with a brief ascent but is not hard after that. It goes very straight to Muthill, where you rejoin the **A822** into Crieff. My B&B, Somerton House, Turret Bank (01764 653513) was in the western part of Crieff and difficult to find so if you decide to stay there (and it is a very nice and comfortable place), take a taxi or arrange to be picked up and returned to the same spot the next morning.

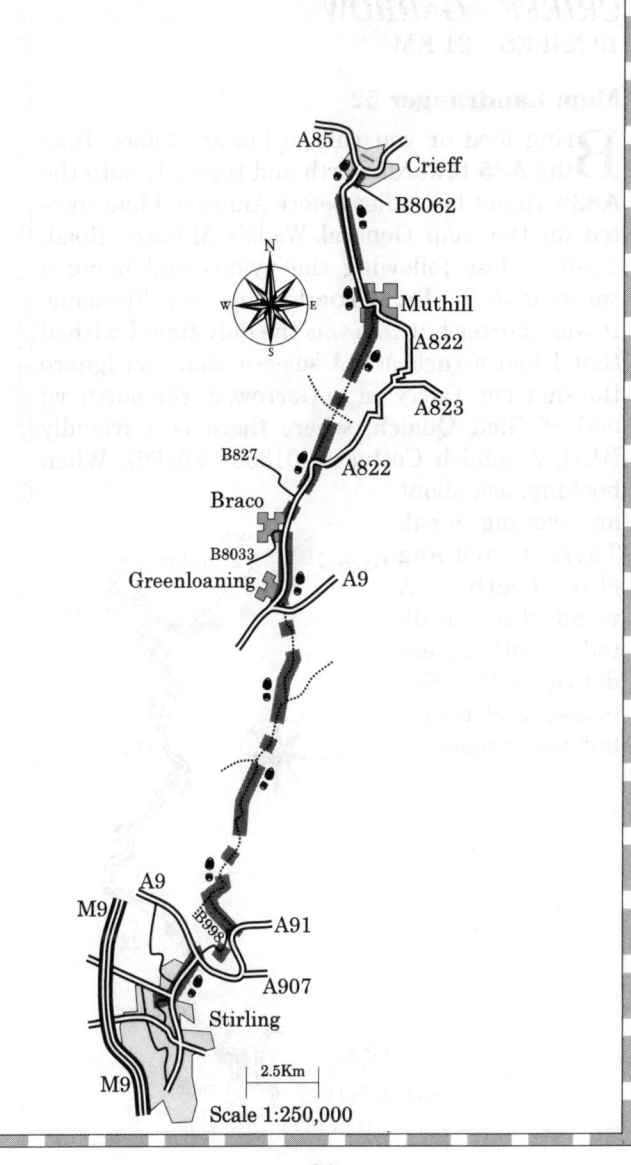

DAY 34.
CRIEFF – GARROW
19 MILES – 31 KM

Map: Landranger 52

Bring food or you will go hungry today. Take the **A85** towards Perth and turn left onto the **A822**. About two miles before Amulree I had spotted on the map General Wade's Military Road, more or less following the pylons and being a shortcut to the **local road** along Loch Freuchie. It was shorter but this was the only time I wished that I had a rucksack. I suggest that you ignore the shortcut. Carry on to Garrow, at the northern end of Glen Quaich, where there is a friendly B&B, 2 Quaich Cottages (01350 725266). When booking, ask about an evening meal. There is nothing else nearby. A wonderful walk today with splendid views. Very few houses and people but many sheep.

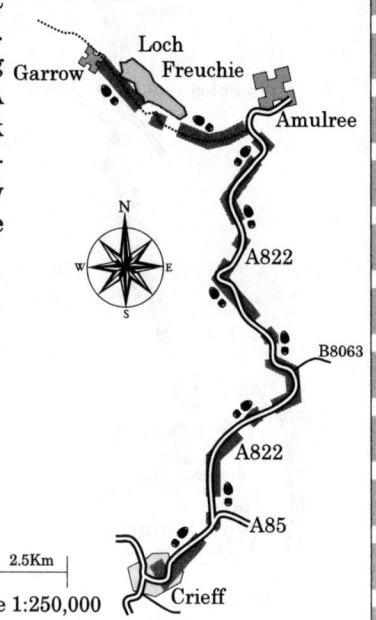

DAY 35.
GARROW – TUMMEL BRIDGE
18 MILES – 29 KM

Map: Landranger 52

Continue on the **local road** which goes steeply uphill for a mile or so and over a beautiful wild landscape to a long descent to the **A827** and Kenmore, where there are eating places and a store. Cross the bridge in Kenmore and turn right onto a **local road** signposted Tummel Bridge and left onto the **B846** to Tummel Bridge. A few miles before reaching Tummel Bridge you will see the geometrical cone of Schiehallion on your left, one of the Munros, i.e. mountain peaks in Scotland over 3,000 feet in height. I recommend a stay at the Heatherbank, Tummel Bridge (01822 634324), where my kind hosts dried my wet clothes and were very helpful in other respects. There is a restaurant quite near.

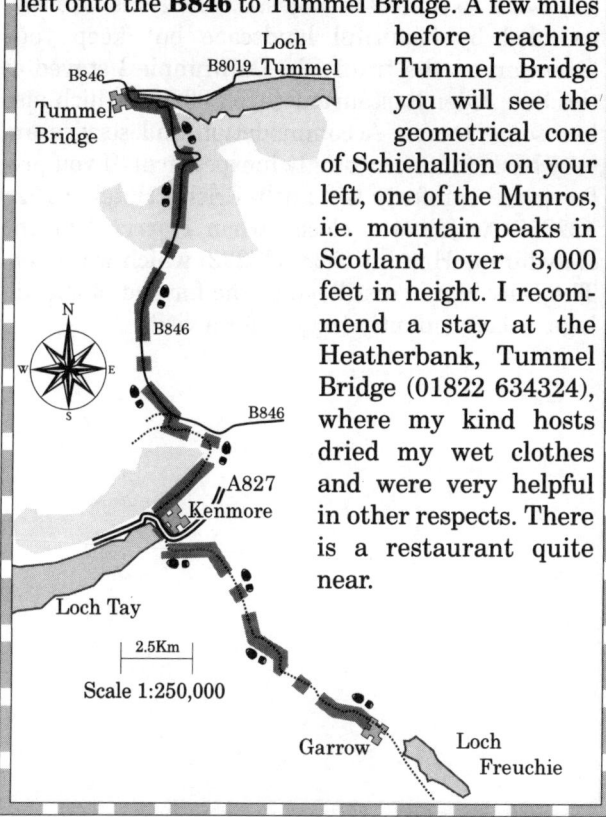

DAY 36.
TUMMEL BRIDGE – DALWHINNIE
25 MILES – 40 KM

Map: Landranger 42

No eating places en route today. Leave Tummel Bridge on the **B846** and after ½ mile turn right onto a **local road** with some good ascents and descents. Turn right again onto the **B847** to Trinafour, left onto a **local road**, and left onto the **A9** and, finally, left onto the **A889** into Dalwhinnie. The walk to the A9 is majestic. The A9 is also surrounded by beautiful landscape but keep your attention on the traffic. In Dalwhinnie I stayed at the Ben Alder Restaurant (0152 83268) which also has some rooms. Accommodation and service are very basic (but accordingly inexpensive). If you prefer more comfort, try Loch Ericht Hotel (01528 522257) which was closed when I arrived or the Dalwhinnie Hotel (01528 522222) which was open. The Dalwhinnie distillery, at the far end of the village, is conveniently located for a visit.

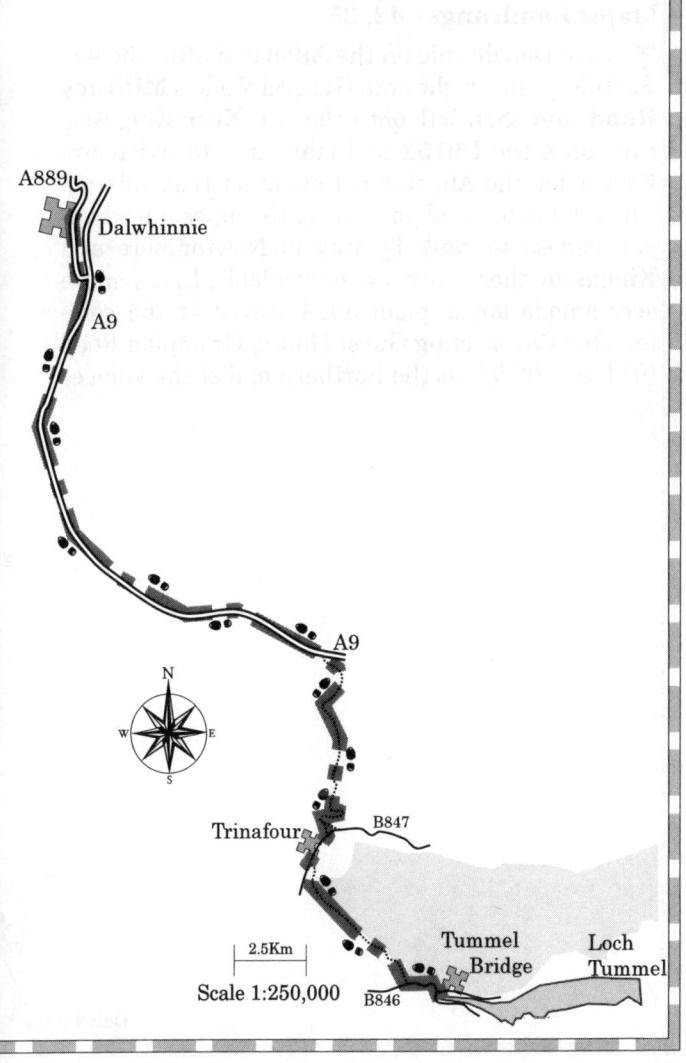

A889

Dalwhinnie

A9

A9

N
W   E
S

Trinafour   B847

2.5Km

Scale 1:250,000

Tummel
Bridge

Loch
Tummel

B846

Maps: Landranger 42, 35

Leave Dalwhinnie on the **A889** and after the distillery turn right onto General Wade's **Military Road** and then left onto the **A9**. Near Kingussie turn onto the **B9152** and stay on it to Aviemore. Except for the A9, this is fine, quiet roadwalking. The road is flat and you eat up the miles quickly. If you choose to walk by way of Newtonmore and Kingussie, there are services available. In Aviemore accommodation is plentiful. I stayed at the comfortable Ravenscraig Guest House, Grampian Road (01479 810278), at the northern end of the village.

A889

Dalwhinnie

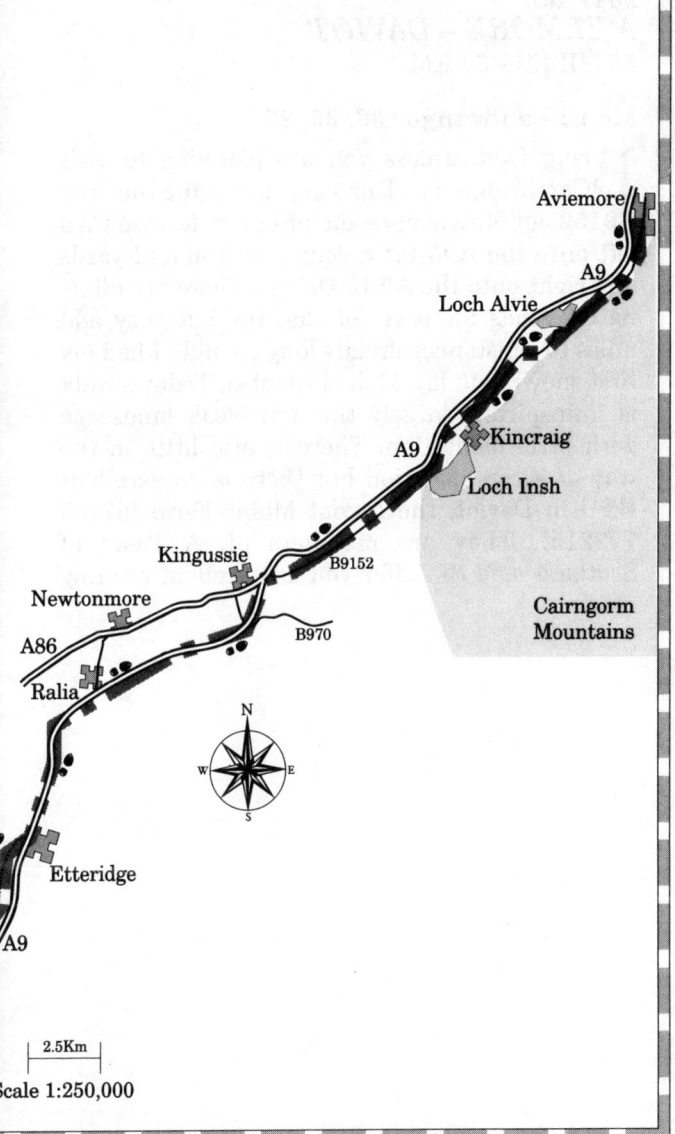

Aviemore

A9

Loch Alvie

Kincraig

A9

Loch Insh

Kingussie

B9152

Newtonmore

A86

B970

Ralia

Cairngorm
Mountains

N
W E
S

Etteridge

A9

| 2.5Km |

Scale 1:250,000

DAY 38.
AVIEMORE – DAVIOT
23 MILES – 37 KM

Maps: Landranger 36, 35, 27

Bring food, unless you are planning to visit Carrbridge or Tomatin. Continue on the **B9152** out of Aviemore and after a mile or so turn left onto the **A95** for a couple of hundred yards and right onto the **A9** to Daviot. There are alternative roads for parts of the way but they add miles to a distance, already long enough. I had my first snowfall today, 11th November. Today's walk is uninspiring, largely through bleak landscape with little habitation. There is also little in the way of accommodation but there is an excellent B&B in Daviot, the Daviot Mains Farm (01463 772215). They are members of 'A Taste of Scotland' and can offer you an excellent evening meal.

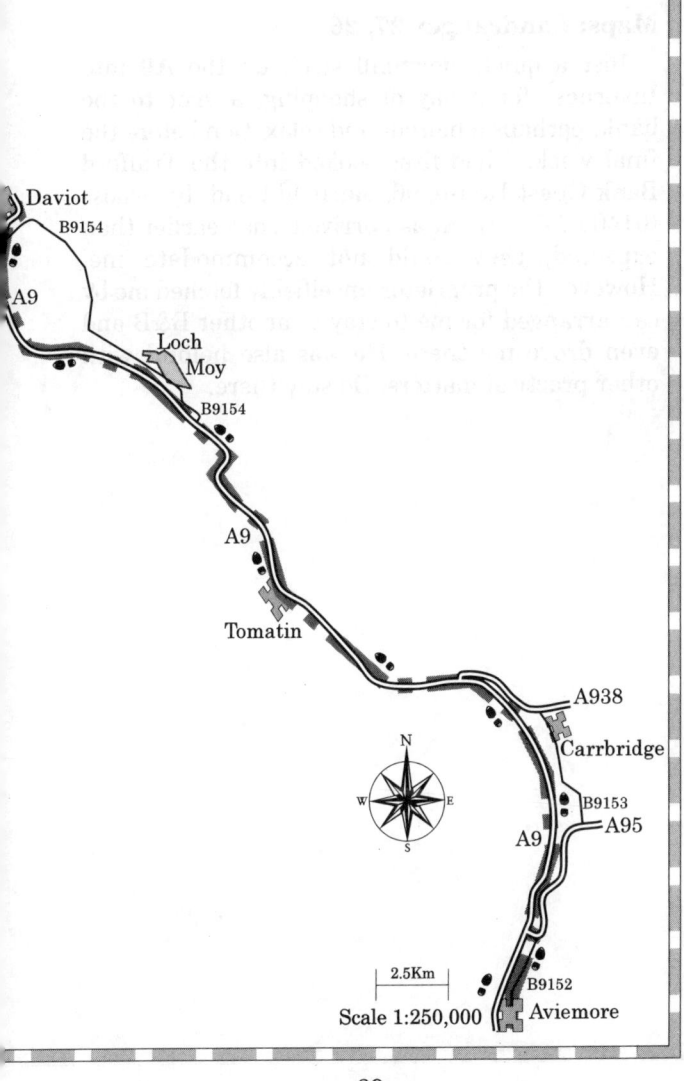

DAY 39.
DAVIOT – INVERNESS
6 MILES – 10 KM

Maps: Landranger 27, 26

Just a quick, downhill stroll on the **A9** into Inverness for a day of shopping, a visit to the bank, perhaps a haircut and relaxation before the final week. I had first booked into the Trafford Bank Guest House, 96, Fairfield Road, Inverness (01463 241414) but as I arrived a day earlier than expected, they could not accommodate me. However, the proprietor unselfishly fetched me by car, arranged for me to stay at another B&B and even drove me there. He was also helpful with other practical matters. Do stay there.

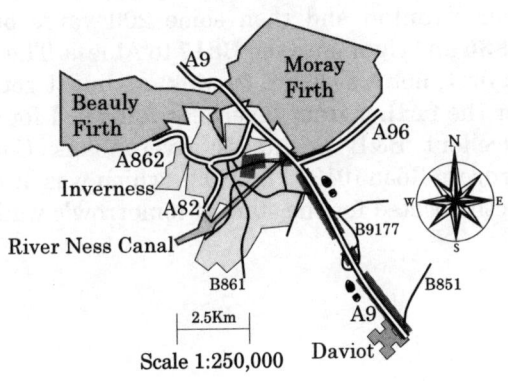

Beauly Firth

Moray Firth

A9

A96

A862

Inverness

A82

River Ness Canal

B9177

B861

B851

A9

N

W E

S

2.5Km

Scale 1:250,000

Daviot

DAY 40.
INVERSNESS – ALNESS
19 MILES – 31 KM

Maps: Landranger 26, 21

There are no eating places or shops until you reach Evanton and Alness. Leave Inverness on the **A9**. At the Kessock Bridge you will see the first signpost to John o' Groats (120 miles). The final countdown can begin. Walk across the Black Isle and cross the Cromarty Firth. After about two miles more on the A9 turn left onto a **local road** over Evanton and then some 200 yards on the **A836** and right onto the **B817** to Alness. The A9 is, at first, not a pleasure to walk on, but it gets better the farther from Inverness you get. I found an excellent B&B in Alness: Averonbank Cottage, Ardross Road (01349 882392), which was also perfectly located for the start of tomorrow's walk.

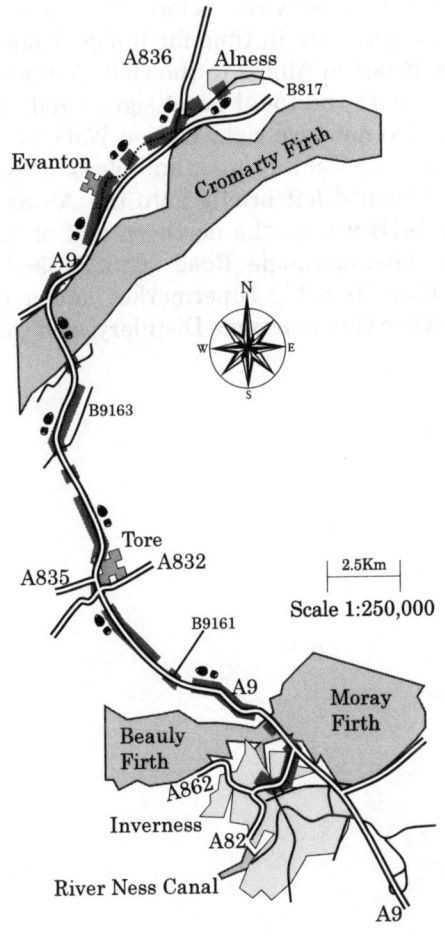

DAY 41.
ALNESS – TAIN
13 MILES – 21 KM

Map: Landranger 21

There are no services before Tain but you should get there in time for lunch. Take the **Ardross Road** in Alness to the Golf Course and turn right onto the **local road** signposted 'Tain 12 miles'. Do not turn right earlier. Walk by way of Scotsburn to Tain. A quiet and pleasant walk. At Tain I turned left briefly onto the **A9** as my pleasant B&B was at the northern end of Tain: Dunbius, Glenmorangie Road (01862 894340). Nearby there is a big supermarket and a mile north lies the Glenmorangie Distillery, well worth visiting.

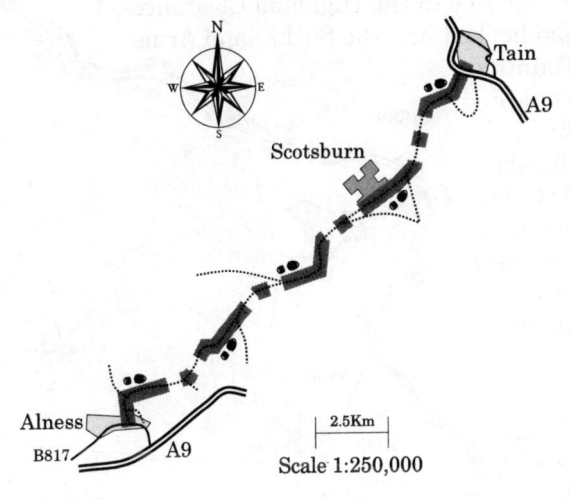

Tain

A9

Scotsburn

N
W E
S

Alness

B817 A9

2.5Km

Scale 1:250,000

DAY 42.
TAIN – BRORA
25 MILES – 40 KM

Maps: Landranger 21, 17

Bring something to eat. Straightforward map-reading: The **A9** all the way to Brora. There seems to be a path along the beach between Golspie and Brora, but I did not use it. The surroundings are attractive enough but walk carefully. The monument you will see on a hilltop, Beinn a' Bhragaidh, as you approach Golspie, is a statue of George Granville Leveson-Gower, the first Duke of Sutherland and infamous for his role in the Highland Clearances. I had booked into the Sutherland Arms, Fountain Square, Brora (01408 621209), where a nice meal can be enjoyed.

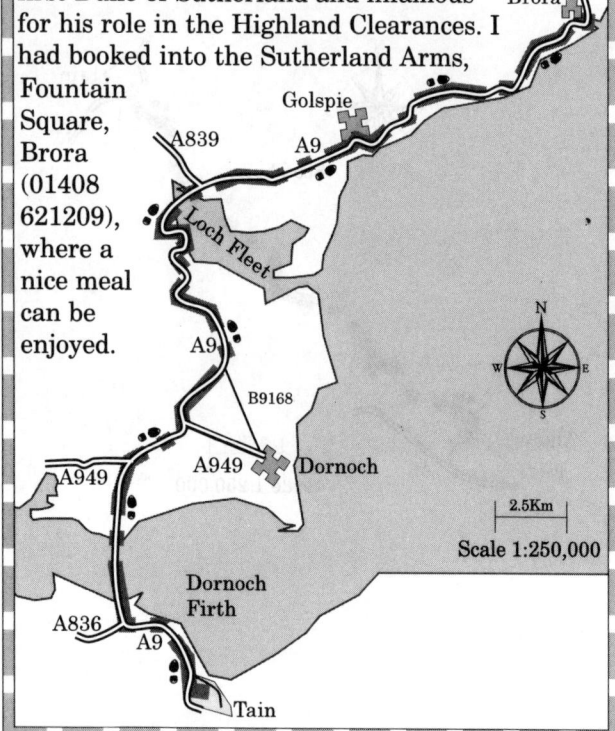

Map: Landranger 17

The **A9** to Helmsdale, and it was not too busy. I stayed in comfort at the Belgrave Arms Hotel, Dunrobin Street, Helmsdale (01431 821242), where there is an excellent restaurant.

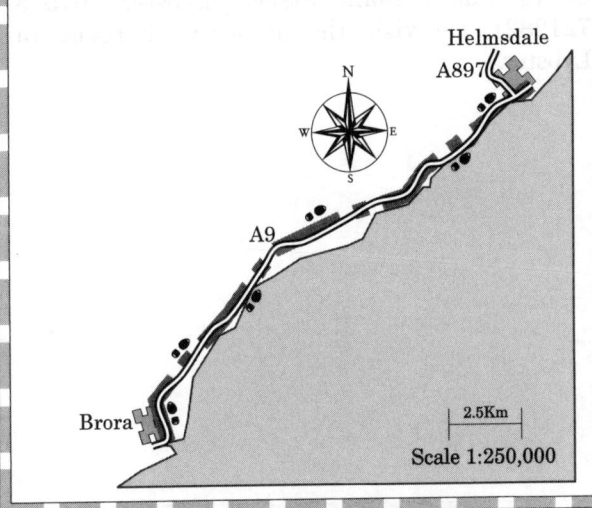

DAY 44.
HELMSDALE – LYBSTER
23 MILES – 37 KM

Maps: Landranger 17, 11

Bring something to eat and drink. Another day without alternatives: The **A9** all the way to Lybster. About four miles after Helmsdale there are steps leading up to a grave with the inscription: 'Wm. Welch perished here 31st January, 1878'. My enquiries revealed that he was a vagabond who, having been turned away from a farm nearby (totally inconsistent with Scottish hospitality), froze to death on this spot. It was discovered that he had thousands of pounds in his pockets! This fortune went to charity. Pay your respects to an unfortunate fellow walker. At Berriedale there are some steep gradients (13%). A pleasant day's walk with splendid views. I found a most friendly B&B at the Bolton House, Greys Place, Main Street, Lybster (01593 721282). Do visit the attractive harbour in Lybster.

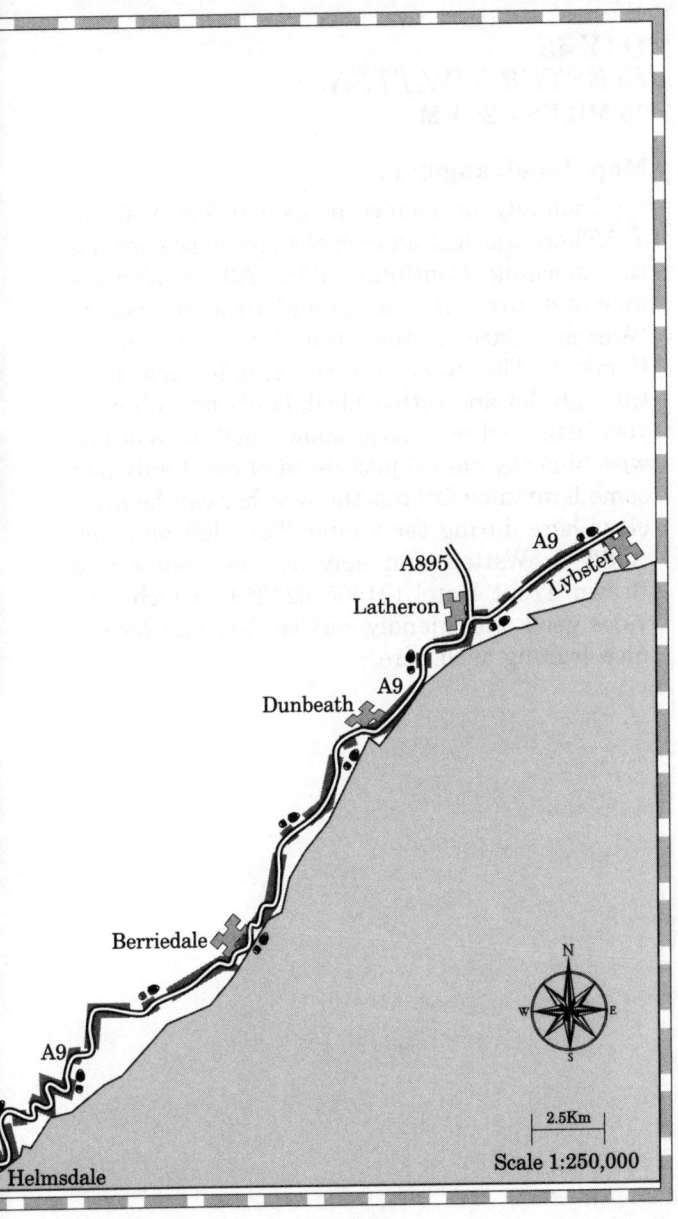

DAY 45.
LYBSTER – WATTEN
15 MILES – 24 KM

Map: Landranger 11

Absolutely no chance of food before Watten. There was half an inch of snow on the ground this morning. Continue on the **A9** for about a mile and turn left onto a **local road** signposted 'Watten'. Gaze at the ancient Grey Cairns of Camster. The road is very straight and runs through flat and rather bleak landscape, offering very little shelter. A large snow cloud in an otherwise blue sky passed just ahead of me. I only had some light snowfall but the weather can be atrocious here during the winter. Turn left onto the **A882** to Watten and stay at the comfortable Brown Trout Hotel (01955 621354), which provides good and friendly service. You can have a nice evening meal here.

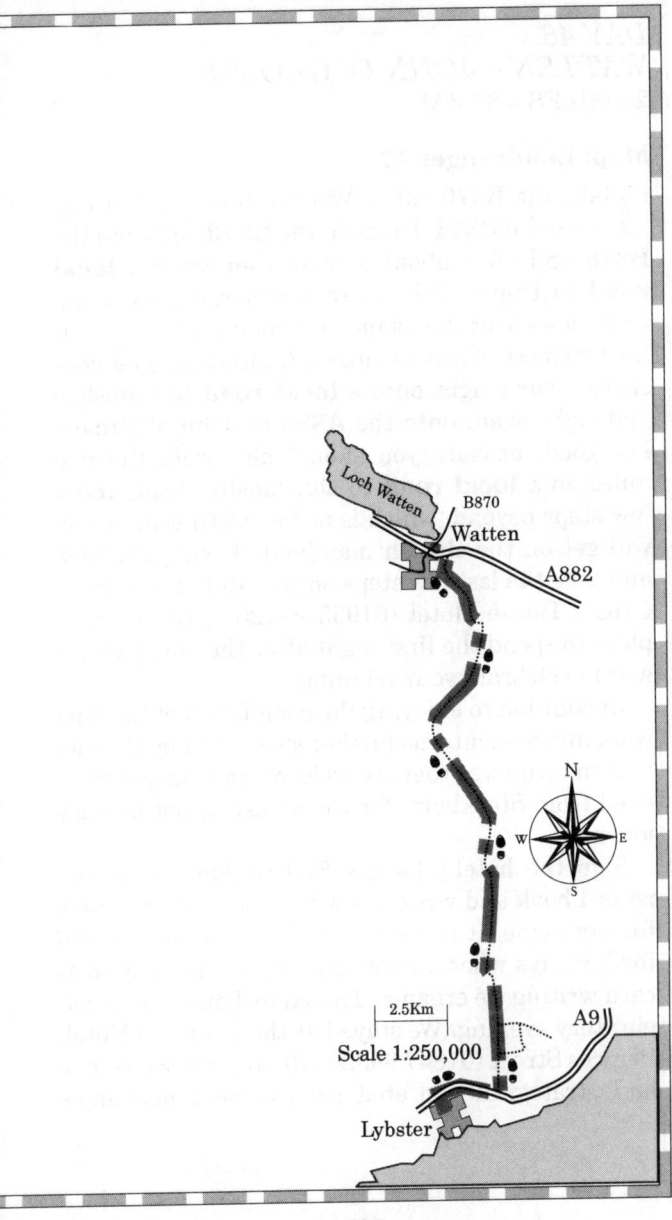

Loch Watten

B870

Watten

A882

N
W   E
S

2.5Km

Scale 1:250,000

A9

Lybster

DAY 46.
WATTEN – JOHN O' GROATS
23 MILES – 37 KM

Map: Landranger 12

Take the **B870** out of Watten, turn right briefly onto the **B874**, left onto the **B870**, left onto the **B876** and after about a mile, right onto a **local road** to Upper Gills. Here a panorama opens up with views over the Island of Stroma and, behind it, the Orkneys. The ultimate destination is so far concealed. Turn right onto a **local road** to Canisbay and right again onto the **A836** to John o' Groats. For good measure you should also walk the two miles on a **local road** to Duncansby Head, and a few steps beyond, which is as far north-east as you will get on the British mainland. Then walk back and take the last few steps on the **A9** to the John o' Groats House Hotel (01955 611203), the obvious place to spend the first night after the long journey and to celebrate your triumph.

In addition to enjoying the completion of the long walk my moment was further sweetened by the fact that my wife was there to welcome me, having travelled from Stockholm for the occasion, not an easy journey.

Sign the hotel's Land's End to John o' Groats record book and write a few bon mots. Do not look for my name. It is not there. The hotel was closed for holidays when I arrived so after a bout of postcard writing we organized a taxi to Thurso for a celebratory evening. We stayed at the Pentland Hotel, Princes Street (01847 893202/3), in the town centre and strategically located for the next morning's

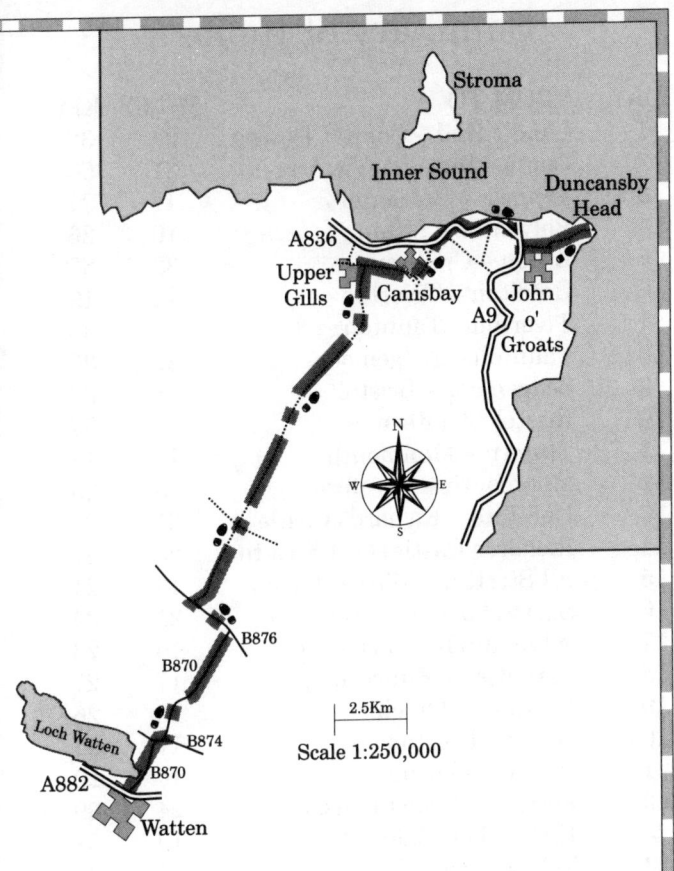

06.30 train departure for Edinburgh. This is the only hotel I have visited which will provide a cooked breakfast at 05.30 a.m!

Summary of Route

DAY	FROM/TO	MILES	KM
1	Land's End – Connor Downs	20	32
2	Connor Downs – Victoria	31	50
3	Victoria – Bolventor	17	27
4	Bolventor – Lifton	16	26
5	Lifton – Crediton	33	53
6	Crediton – Tiverton	12	19
7	Tiverton – Taunton	22	35
8	Taunton – Sedgemoor	22	35
9	Sedgemoor – Bristol	23	37
10	Bristol – Tintern	23	37
11	Tintern – Monmouth	11	18
12	Monmouth – Hereford	18	29
13	Hereford – Richards Castle	21	34
14	Richards Castle – All Stretton	20	32
15	All Stretton – Shrewsbury	13	21
16	Shrewsbury – Whitchurch	21	34
17	Whitchurch – Tarporley	16	26
18	Tarporley – Runcorn	17	27
19	Runcorn – Orrell	16	26
20	Orrell – Preston	17	27
21	Preston – Forton	14	23
22	Forton – Kirkby Lonsdale	24	39
23	Kirkby Lonsdale – Tebay	19	31
24	Tebay – Penrith	19	31
25	Penrith – Carlisle	17	27
26	Carlisle – Eaglesfield	24	39
27	Eaglesfield – Boreland	12	19
28	Boreland – Moffat	12	19
29	Moffat – Abington	17	27
30	Abington – Larkhall	21	34
31	Larkhall – Kilsyth	24	39
32	Kilsyth – Stirling	13	21
33	Stirling – Crieff	20	32

DAY	FROM/TO	MILES	KM
34	Crieff – Garrow	19	31
35	Garrow – Tummel Bridge	18	29
36	Tummel Bridge – Dalwhinnie	25	40
37	Dalwhinnie – Aviemore	28	45
38	Aviemore – Daviot	23	37
39	Daviot – Inverness	6	10
40	Inverness – Alness	19	31
41	Alness – Tain	13	21
42	Tain – Brora	25	40
43	Brora – Helmsdale	12	19
44	Helmsdale – Lybster	23	37
45	Lybster – Watten	15	24
46	Watten – John o' Groats	23	37
	TOTAL DISTANCE	874	1406
	DAILY AVERAGE	19	31

The above distances are approximations and some of them may be on the conservative side. Furthermore, strolls to shops, restaurants and sightseeing are not included and will increase the daily distance by perhaps 1-2 miles.

Epilogue

Was it worth it all? I will not deny that there were a few times when I cursed myself for having taken on the walk but I never seriously considered calling the whole thing off.

I encountered some appalling weather during the second part of the journey. There were a few days with heavy rain and gale force winds with gusts that nearly propelled me into the ditch or forced me to run to avoid falling flat on my face. I think that I experienced almost the whole range of British weather, good as well as bad, with the exception of a blizzard.

My most humbling moments came some miles after Abington when a violent hail-storm came out of the blue. There was a clap of thunder and an ominous cloud approached me rapidly. I tried to reach a house I saw some distance ahead but did not make it. Everything went white around me and the strength of the wind peppering me with hail-stones forced me down on all fours, trying to find some shelter behind my trolley. Luckily the hail-storm was of short duration and after a while there was even some sunshine. The outburst was very local and I was probably the only one it hit. I wonder why I was singled out. The house I had seen, and which was apparently closed for the season so I could not get in to change my soaked things in comfort, turned out to be named, perhaps appropriately, the Black Sheep Inn. I mention this little incident to underline the need to have respect for British weather.

I never lost a day because of the weather but there were a few days when it would perhaps have been cosier to hole up with a good book in a nice B&B but I was impatient to get on with it.

But do not let me discourage you! On many days the weather was fine, if often fairly cold – there was even some snow in northern Scotland – and several days were glorious and made walking in the often lovely landscape a sheer delight.

Another factor which made the walk a pleasant experience was the friendliness of the people, not only where I stayed overnight, but in general. Motorists often honked their horn or gave me a friendly wave. I was several times offered a lift, which I of course had to decline as I would not cheat a single inch, but there were occasions with foul weather when I was sorely tempted.

I was stopped several times by motorists who enquired about the way and I suppose that my map-case inspired confidence. Being a tourist I was of course flattered, pleased to have a chat and often able to help out. I was, however, nonplussed when a lady in Ludlow asked for directions to the nearest bicycle shop.

I had expected to meet a number of interesting and eccentric 'End to End' walkers on the road with whom to chat and share experiences but the fact is that I did not meet one single long distance walker on the whole journey. It is true that I walked in the low-season and by road, but really...

The only notable walker I encountered on the road was Paul whom I met near Kirkby Lonsdale. His hobby was to collect pubs. Most weekends he took the train or car to a new area and visited as many pubs as possible on foot. He had a glass of ale in each pub, recorded his impressions of the place and usually took a photograph. He had been at it for some 25 years and visited around 10,000 pubs! A commendable and no doubt highly rewarding pursuit. I think of him as pub-crawl Paul.

The 'End to End' walk is a crash fitness course

and it was a pleasure to be able gradually to walk without really feeling tired. I believe that in the last few weeks of the walk I could have increased the daily mileage considerably without feeling exhausted but after the sad experiences resulting from the second and fifth day I did not really trust my Achilles tendons and therefore kept to a restrained mileage. Besides, the days were getting shorter.

In the course of a long journey like this somehow walking becomes a way of life and feels very satisfying. Whilst I was certainly looking forward to completing the walk, in a way there was an element of regret when it was all over. But then, there is always the possibility of doing an encore.

So, was it worth it all? My answer to that question is YES! It is a unique experience and the many memories will last a lifetime. The main difficulty is to take that first step, i.e. to decide to make the journey. Good luck!

Further Reading

The only books I have found about walking the whole way by road are the ones by Noel Blackham and Richard Brown but all the books listed below should be inspirational and of interest whether you are planning to actually do the walk or just wish to make an armchair journey.

A Grandparents' Guide from Land's End to John o' Groats
by Eileen and Herbert Witherington. Wande Publications, 38 North Guards, Whitburn, Sunderland SR6 7AD (1993).

One man and his dog go walkies. John o' Groats to Land's End
by Noel Blackham. World Musicals, 28 Wilsford Green, Edgbaston, Birmingham B15 3UG (1991).

Journey through Britain
by John Hillaby. Constable and Company Ltd., 3 The Lanchesters, 162 Fulham Palace Road, London W6 9ER (1968). Paperback edition 1995.

Land's End to John o' Groats. A choice of footpaths for walking the length of Britain
by Andrew McCloy. Hodder and Stoughton, A division of Hodder Headline PLC, 338 Euston Road, London NW1 3BH (1994).

The Winning Experience
by Richard Brown. Institute of Human Development, Burnts House, Chelwood, BS18 4NL (1996).

End to End Stuff
by John Simcock. Avon Books, 1 Dovedale Studios, 465 Battersea Park Road, London SW11 4LR (1996).